Daily Literacy Activities

19ᵀᴴ CENTURY AMERICAN HISTORY

REM 391

AUTHOR: Sue LaRoy

A TEACHING RESOURCE FROM

www.rempub.com

REMEDIA PUBLICATIONS, INC.
SCOTTSDALE, AZ

This product utilizes innovative strategies and proven methods to improve student learning. The product is based upon reliable research and effective practices that have been replicated in classrooms across the United States. Information regarding the Common Core State Standards this product meets is available at www.rempub.com/standards.

Table of Contents

Teacher Guide

Literacy means having the ability to read and write. Literacy also means having knowledge or competency in a specified area. The goal of this book is to help students improve reading and writing skills as they learn important information about 19th Century American history. If students can successfully read each story in the book, understand the historical facts presented, and then write about what they have learned, they will have become more literate in American history.

The format of this book lends itself to use with students who are functioning below grade level. The information is presented in a way that allows for differentiated instruction. Teacher understanding of a student's ability level will help determine how much material a student can successfully complete in an allotted time on a daily basis. To help keep track of when each part of the lesson is completed, each page has a line for writing the current date.

BOOK FORMAT

The 14 stories in this book take students on a journey that begins with the Lewis and Clark Expedition and ends with the Civil War, Reconstruction, and the last of the Indian Wars. Each three-part story, complete with historical images, is accompanied by five skill-based reading and writing activity pages. These eight pages form a study unit for each story. The stories are numbered to help keep all the story components together.

To encourage students to read and then re-read the text, there is a "locating the information" activity at the bottom of each story page. This simple exercise helps to reinforce key facts from the story. Each story includes words which many students may find challenging. Use of these words is necessary in order to convey historical accuracy. There are three "Words to Know" pages that list difficult or unfamiliar words. Three "People and Places" pages list the names of important people and historic places mentioned in the stories. Two pages of "Enrichment Ideas" offer suggestions for discussion, research, and higher level comprehension questions. The Answer Key provides answers for the comprehension and cloze activity pages.

READABILITY

A specific challenge for this book was being true to history while simplifying the content. An effort was made to create stories that were rich with important historical information, yet on a level that would be understood by those students reading below grade level.

To accomplish this, short sentences, simple explanations, and plenty of repetition were used whenever possible. A reading specialist reviewed the stories for content and reading ease. Use of the historically relevant vocabulary resulted in an average reading level ranging from 4.0 to 5.5 according to the Flesch-Kincaid Scale. The interest level is grade 5 and up.

SUGGESTIONS FOR USE

Start by assembling one of the eight-page study units into a folder with the "Words to Know" and "People and Places" lists for that story. Pre-reading strategies can be used based on each student's needs.

Pre-Reading Strategies

Have the student read the title and study the three images on the story pages. Ask the student what the story might be about. On a sheet of paper, make two columns. One labeled "What I Know" and one labeled "What I Want to Know." Anything the student knows about the topic can be written in one column, and anything the student would like to know can be written in the second column. This may pique interest and give the student a reason to read the story. Point out the "Words to Know" and "People and Places" lists that correspond to the story. Ask the student to identify any unfamiliar words. Talk about the historic figures and groups of people mentioned in the story. Offer help with understanding and the pronunciation of difficult words.

Have students create flashcards for difficult words and allow them to work in pairs to master the words. Some students may benefit from learning the definitions of the words and using them in sentences. Dictionary apps are available for a variety of digital devices that allow students to listen to the definition and pronunciation of a word.

To help set the stage for the story, discuss the countries, regions, colonies, states, and cities referred to in the story. Use either a current or historic map to point out the locations.

Daily Activities

Daily literacy activities presented in small increments can allow individual students to proceed at their own pace often resulting in a greater understanding of the subject matter.

For example:

Day 1: Student reads the first page of the story and completes the "locating the answer" activity.

Day 2: Student reviews the first page of the story and completes the comprehension questions for that page.

Day 3: Student reads the second page of the story and completes the "locating the answer" activity.

Day 4: Student reviews the second page of the story and completes the comprehension questions for that page.

Day 5: Student reads the third page of the story and completes the "locating the answer" activity.

Day 6: Student reviews the third page of the story and completes the comprehension questions for that page.

Day 7: Student completes the cloze activity and then writes a short summary of the topics listed on the final activity page.

This timeline and the amount of material assigned each day can be adjusted based on skill level. The story sections make excellent homework assignments.

Post-Reading

After completing a study unit, ask students to compare what they have learned with what they wanted to know about the topic. Unanswered questions can stimulate further research.

The two enrichment pages offer ideas to extend learning and help students gain a deeper understanding of the topics in this book.

Lewis and Clark Expedition: The Beginning

The Louisiana Purchase

In 1801, Thomas Jefferson became the third president of the United States. His main goal was to increase the size of the country. At that time, the United States territory ended at the Mississippi River. Jefferson had a dream. He wanted the United States to stretch from coast to coast. He wanted it to take up the entire continent.

The land west of the Mississippi River was called the Louisiana Territory. It was owned by France. The territory included 827,000 square miles. The land started at the Gulf of Mexico. It went north all the way to the Canadian border. It went west to the Rocky Mountains. Jefferson wanted this territory for the United States. In 1803, he bought the Louisiana Territory from the French for $15 million. This was known as the Louisiana Purchase.

There wasn't much known about this vast land. Native American tribes lived throughout the territory. But only a few European fur trappers had ever been there. There were no maps to follow.

Jefferson was eager for this new territory to be explored. He thought there might be a water route between the Mississippi River and the Pacific Ocean. Boats could be used to make the journey. This would open up the west to the fur trade and settlements. It would allow the nation to grow.

1. Underline the two sentences that tell what Jefferson's dream was.

2. Underline the sentence that tells how much was paid for the Louisiana Purchase.

3. Underline the sentence that tells what Jefferson thought there might be in the new territory.

Name_____ Date _9/29/21_

Answer the questions with complete sentences.

1. What was Jefferson's main goal as president of the United States?

   He wanted the U.S.A to go from east to west.

2. Who owned the Louisiana Territory?

   The French owned the ~~territory~~ louisiana Territory.

3. How much was paid to buy the Louisiana Territory?

   Jefferson ~~~~ paid Fifteen Million dollers.

4. Who lived in the Louisiana Territory?

   The Native Americans lived in the Louisiana Territory.

5. What did Jefferson think might be found in the new territory?

   He thought there might be a water-way that led to the Pacific Ocean.

The Corps of Discovery

Story 1

Jefferson decided to send an expedition to find a route through the new territory. This would be a big challenge. There were many dangers to be faced. Thousands of miles of unmapped land would have to be crossed. It was unknown if the Native Americans would be friendly. He needed a group of young men who were strong and brave. He needed men who could survive in the wilderness. Jefferson would call his expedition the Corps (kor) of Discovery.

Jefferson asked his personal secretary, Meriwether Lewis, to lead the expedition. Lewis was only 30 years old. But he was an expert outdoorsman. Jefferson trusted him. He thought Lewis was a smart, brave person. Lewis would choose the men for the Corps.

Meriwether Lewis

Meriwether Lewis was born in Virginia in 1774. In 1793, he graduated from college. Then he joined the Virginia militia. Next Lewis became a captain in the U.S. Army. He was very excited to be chosen as the leader of the expedition. He asked his best friend, William Clark, to join him.

William Clark

William Clark was four years older than Lewis. He was also born in Virginia. Later he moved to Kentucky and joined the Kentucky militia. Then he joined the U.S. Army where he met Lewis. Clark had spent a lot of time in the wilderness. He was happy to be a part of this big adventure.

1. Underline the sentence that tells why Jefferson decided to send an expedition.
2. Underline the sentence that tells who Jefferson asked to lead the expedition.
3. Underline the sentence that tells who Lewis asked to join him.

Answer the questions with complete sentences.

1. What did Jefferson call his expedition?

   _____

   _____

2. Who did Jefferson ask to lead the expedition?

   _____

   _____

3. What did Jefferson think of Meriwether Lewis?

   _____

   _____

4. Who did Lewis ask to join him on the expedition?

   _____

   _____

5. Where did Lewis and Clark meet?

   _____

   _____

Preparing for the Trip

Story 1

Lewis asked Clark to be his co-captain. He needed Clark's help. They would lead the expedition together. The expedition became known as the Lewis and Clark Expedition. A group of about 40 men were chosen for the trip. The men were all good hunters and outdoorsmen. The oldest was 35 and the youngest was 17. The group planned for the trip and trained for several months. The men built up their strength. They practiced survival skills. They made boats for river travel.

Lewis knew there would be many hardships and challenges. He wanted to be prepared for anything. Lewis trained with the top scientists in the country. He studied botany and zoology. He would keep a record of all the plants and animals they found along the way. He studied astronomy and map-making skills. He learned about medicine from the most famous doctor of the time.

Supplies were carefully selected. Lewis bought food, clothing, camping equipment, medicine, rifles, and special map-making tools. He also bought gifts for the Native American tribes they would meet. He hoped the tribes would be friendly. The gifts included knives, tobacco, mirrors, beads, and brightly colored cloth. When Lewis was done, over 3,500 pounds of supplies had been purchased! Soon it would time to start their journey.

1. Underline the sentence that tells what the expedition became known as.

2. Underline the sentence that tells who Lewis trained with.

3. Underline the sentence that tells what gifts Lewis bought for the Native American tribes he would meet.

Answer the questions with complete sentences.

1. What did the expedition become known as?

   _____

   _____

2. How did the men chosen for the expedition train for the trip?

   _____

   _____

3. Name two ways Lewis prepared for the trip.

   _____

   _____

4. What kind of supplies did Lewis buy for the trip?

   _____

   _____

5. Who did Lewis buy gifts for?

   _____

   _____

Complete each sentence with a word from the box.

expedition	increase	France
expert	best	supplies
months	maps	learned

1. Jefferson's main goal was to _____ the size of the United States.

2. The Louisiana Territory was owned by _____.

3. There were no _____ of the Louisiana Territory.

4. Jefferson would call his _____ the Corps of Discovery.

5. Meriwether Lewis was an _____ outdoorsman.

6. Lewis asked his _____ friend, William Clark, to join him.

7. The group planned and trained for the trip for several _____.

8. Lewis _____ about medicine from the most famous doctor of the time.

9. Over 3,500 pounds of _____ were purchased for the trip.

Read each completed sentence to make sure it makes sense.

Write two or more sentences about each topic.

Louisiana Territory

_____

_____

_____

_____

Meriwether Lewis

_____

_____

_____

_____

William Clark

_____

_____

_____

_____

Lewis and Clark Expedition: The Journey

Meriwether Lewis and William Clark had a mission to explore the unknown Louisiana Territory. This vast territory was a mystery. They had no maps to follow. They did not know what to expect. Lewis and Clark hoped to discover a route west to the Pacific Ocean.

The Journey Begins

After months of preparation, Lewis decided it was time to start the expedition. Lewis and Clark had a team of about 40 men to go with them.

On May 14, 1804, the group left St. Louis, Missouri. They started out on the Missouri River in three boats. The largest boat was a 55-foot keelboat. It was a large wooden riverboat. There was a cabin in the center. It held most of their supplies. It took 22 men to row the boat. The other two boats were smaller. They were built like canoes. The rest of the men traveled in them.

Traveling on the Missouri River was very difficult. Sometimes the boats had to be pulled over rocks and rough spots. Lots of mosquitoes and ticks bothered the men every day. Lewis hoped the river would eventually lead them to the Rocky Mountains.

By August of 1804, the expedition had made it to South Dakota. They stayed for awhile to hunt buffalo and other wild game. They met some Native Americans from the Plains tribes. Some were friendly. Some were not.

1. Underline the sentence that tells what Lewis and Clark hoped to discover.
2. Underline the sentence that tells when the group left on their journey.
3. Underline the sentence that tells what it was like to travel on the Missouri River.

Answer the questions with complete sentences.

1. What was Lewis and Clark's mission?

   _____

   _____

2. Where did Lewis and Clark begin their journey?

   _____

   _____

3. How big was the largest boat and what was it used for?

   _____

   _____

4. Why was it difficult traveling on the Missouri River?

   _____

   _____

5. Where had the expedition made it to by August of 1804?

   _____

   _____

The First Winter

By November of 1804, the expedition had moved on to central North Dakota. The Mandan people lived there. Lewis and Clark made friends with the Mandan. They gave them gifts. They smoked the peace pipe with the leaders of the tribe.

Winters in North Dakota were very harsh. Lewis and Clark decided to stay until spring. The team built a fort to live in over the winter. It was called Fort Mandan. They stayed for five months. During that time, the men kept busy. They built canoes, made ropes and leather clothing. They learned from the Mandan about the land that was ahead of them.

Sacagawea

Sacagawea was an 18-year-old Shoshone girl. She had been kidnapped from her tribe when she was 12. Then she was sold to her French husband. Lewis and Clark met Sacagawea and her husband at the fort. Her husband was hired to join the expedition. Sacagawea and her two-month-old baby boy were allowed to come along. Lewis thought she could help the team.

The expedition was headed to the Rocky Mountains. The Shoshone lived near there. Sacagawea could be a guide. She could talk with the Shoshone. She would be able to get the horses they needed. Sacagawea was a very smart and brave girl. She became an important member of the expedition.

1. Underline the sentence that tells who lived in central North Dakota.
2. Underline the sentence that tells what the team built to live in over the winter.
3. Underline the sentence that tells who Sacagawea was.

Answer the questions with complete sentences.

1. Who did Lewis and Clark make friends with when they got to North Dakota?

   _____

   _____

2. What was the fort called that the team built?

   _____

   _____

3. What did the men do over the winter to keep busy?

   _____

   _____

4. Who was Sacagawea?

   _____

   _____

5. How could Sacagawea help the expedition?

   _____

   _____

The Next Part of the Journey

The expedition left Fort Mandan in April of 1805. They continued traveling on the Missouri River. When they got to Idaho, they met up with the Shoshone. Sacagawea was very happy to see her people again. Her brother had become chief of the tribe. Because Sacagawea was with the group, her brother helped them.

The journey over the Rocky Mountains was long and dangerous. The weather was freezing. There was not much to eat. The men were starving. Finally, they made it to the other side of the mountains. They found the Snake River. There was salmon and wild game to eat. The men got their strength back. They built five canoes to continue their journey.

The Snake River took them to the Columbia River. The Columbia River took them to the Pacific Ocean. On November 7, 1805, the expedition had reached its destination! The team was thrilled and relieved. Somehow they had made it! They built another fort to live in for the winter. It was called Fort Clatsop.

The Return Journey

On September 23, 1806 the team returned to St. Louis. Huge crowds greeted them. It had taken almost 2½ years to complete the journey. But the expedition was a great success! Lewis and Clark brought back detailed descriptions of all the plants and animals they had seen. They brought back maps of the route. Now other people would be able to find their way out west!

1. Underline the sentence that tells who the expedition met up with in Idaho.
2. Underline the sentence that tells what they found on the other side of the mountains.
3. Underline the sentence that tells how long it took to complete the journey.

Answer the questions with complete sentences.

1. When did the expedition leave Fort Mandan?

   _____

   _____

2. Why did Sacagawea's brother help the expedition?

   _____

   _____

3. How did the men get their strength back after they crossed the mountains?

   _____

   _____

4. Where did the Columbia River take the expedition?

   _____

   _____

5. What did Lewis and Clark bring back from the trip?

   _____

   _____

Complete each sentence with a word from the box.

reached	fort	mystery
met	Shoshone	journey
Mandan	complete	brother

1. The vast Louisiana Territory was a _____.

2. The _____ started out on the Missouri River.

3. The expedition _____ some Native Americans from the Plains tribes.

4. The _____ people lived in central North Dakota.

5. The team built a _____ to live in over the winter.

6. Sacagawea was an 18-year-old _____ girl.

7. Sacagawea's _____ had become chief of the tribe.

8. On November 7, 1805, the expedition _____ the Pacific Ocean.

9. It took almost 2 ½ years to _____ the journey.

Read each completed sentence to make sure it makes sense.

Write two or more sentences about each topic.

Sacagawea

_____

_____

_____

_____

Fort Mandan

_____

_____

_____

_____

The Rocky Mountains

_____

_____

_____

_____

The War of 1812

Causes of the War

For many years, Great Britain had the largest and most powerful navy in the world. It had the most ships. Britain wanted to control the shipping trade. The new country of America started building ships. By the early 1800s, America had more ships than Great Britain. The American ships were used to trade goods with other countries.

Britain did not like this. Britain's navy began to attack American ships at sea. British sailors took American cargo. Sometimes they sunk American ships. They took American sailors from their ships. The American sailors were forced to serve in the British navy. This made the American government very angry.

The British government also wanted to stop Americans from settling in the Ohio River Valley. Native Americans already lived in this large territory. They did not want American settlers taking their land. British leaders in Canada decided to help the Native Americans. The British gave the native tribes rifles to attack the settlers. The settlers thought this was very unfair. It began to feel like the British were attacking them. The settlers asked the U.S. government for help. It was another reason for Americans to be angry with the British.

1. Underline the sentence that tells what the American ships were used for.
2. Underline the sentence that tells what happened to American sailors after they were taken from their ships.
3. Underline the sentence that tells how the British helped the Native Americans.

Name_____ Date_____

Answer the questions with complete sentences.

1. What was America using their ships for?

   _____

   _____

2. What did the British do to American sailors?

   _____

   _____

3. How did the American government feel about what the British were doing to American ships and sailors?

   _____

   _____

4. Why did the British help the Native Americans who lived in the Ohio River Valley?

   _____

   _____

5. Who did the settlers ask for help?

   _____

   _____

Beginning of the War

In 1812, James Madison was the president of the United States. At first, he did not want to go to war with Great Britain. He wasn't sure the American army and navy were ready. The British forces were larger. They had much better training. Madison was worried America could not win another war with Britain. Congress voted to give money to build up the army and navy. Then, on June 18, 1812, Congress voted to go to war with Britain. By this time, Madison agreed.

The first move against Britain was to attack the British colony of Canada. The U.S. thought they could defeat the British troops there. The attack did not go well. The generals leading the attack did not have much experience. The U.S. troops were unprepared. They ran out of supplies. They were easily beaten by the British troops.

In 1813, the U.S. won a couple of important victories. One was the Battle of Lake Erie. This gave America control of the Northwest Territory. The U.S. Navy also won some battles with the British Royal Navy. This caused the British to fight back even harder. They sent more troops to the east coast of America.

British ships sailed into Chesapeake Bay. On August 24, 1814, British troops captured Washington, D.C. They took control of America's capital city. Many government buildings were burned, including the White House!

1. Underline the sentence that tells what the Congress did on June 18, 1812.

2. Underline the sentences that tell why the attack on Canada did not go well.

3. Underline the two sentences that tells what happened after the British took control of America's capital city.

Answer the questions with complete sentences.

1. When did Congress vote to go to war with Britain?

   _____

   _____

2. Why did America's attack on Canada not go well?

   _____

   _____

3. What happened after the Battle of Lake Erie?

   _____

   _____

4. What did the British do when the Americans started to win some battles?

   _____

   _____

5. What happened after the British took control of Washington, D.C.?

   _____

   _____

The Battle of Baltimore

Fort McHenry was in the port city of Baltimore, Maryland. The British thought if they could take the fort, they could win the war. On September 13, 1814, British war ships started firing rockets and cannonballs at the fort. This went on for 25 hours! They hoped the soldiers would panic and leave the fort. But the American patriots

did not give up! They fired their own cannons back at the British ships. The attack had failed. The British left. This American victory was a turning point in the war.

Francis Scott Key watched as Fort McHenry was attacked. After the battle, he saw the American flag flying over the fort. Key wrote a poem about what happened. The poem was called "The Star Spangled Banner." It became the U.S. national anthem.

End of the War

Both the British and the Americans wanted the war to end. They were tired of fighting. Men from both sides met in Ghent, Belgium. On December 24, 1814, a peace treaty was signed. It was called the Treaty of Ghent.

In January of 1815, the Battle of New Orleans took place. News of the peace treaty had not yet reached America. Andrew Jackson led the U.S. troops. They defended the city of New Orleans from the British. Jackson won a big victory. Over 2,000 British soldiers were killed.

Both sides claimed they won the war. But neither side really won or lost anything. However, the signing of the treaty did create a lasting peace between the U.S. and Great Britain.

1. Underline the sentence that tells how long the British fired on Fort McHenry.

2. Underline the sentence that tells when the peace treaty was signed.

3. Underline the sentence that tells why the Battle of New Orleans took place.

Answer the questions with complete sentences.

1. Why did the British want to take Fort McHenry?

   _____

   _____

2. How long did the British fire on Fort McHenry?

   _____

   _____

3. Who wrote a poem about the attack on Fort McHenry?

   _____

   _____

4. Why did the Americans and British decide to end the war?

   _____

   _____

5. Who won a big victory in the Battle of New Orleans?

   _____

   _____

Complete each sentence with a word from the box.

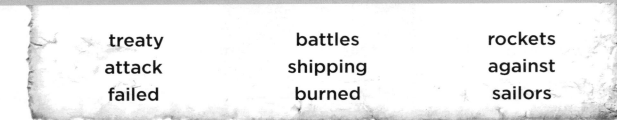

treaty	battles	rockets
attack	shipping	against
failed	burned	sailors

1. Great Britain wanted to control the _____ trade.

2. American _____ were forced to serve in the British navy.

3. The British gave the native tribes rifles to _____ the settlers.

4. America's first move _____ Britain was to attack Canada.

5. America won some _____ with the British navy.

6. The British _____ the White House.

7. The British fired _____ and cannonballs at Fort McHenry.

8. The attack on Fort McHenry _____ .

9. The peace _____ was signed on December 24, 1814.

Read each completed sentence to make sure it makes sense.

Write two or more sentences about each topic.

James Madison

_____

_____

_____

_____

Battle of Baltimore

_____

_____

_____

_____

Battle of New Orleans

_____

_____

_____

_____

The Indian Removal Act

Settlers from Europe started coming to America in the 1600s. They met native people who were already living there. The Europeans called these native people Indians. These early settlers weren't sure what to do about the Indians. Some settlers made friends with the native people. At first, many native tribes helped the settlers. But the settlers wanted their land. It was land that the tribes had been living on for hundreds of years. The tribes did not want to give it up. This caused trouble between the early settlers and the native tribes. There were battles over the land. Many people on both sides were killed.

During the early 1800s, millions of European settlers came to America. They mostly settled along the east coast. Many of the settlers in the southeast were farmers. They wanted the best land for their farms.

At that time, about 125,000 Native Americans lived in the southeastern part of the United States. The main tribes were the Choctaw, Chickasaw, Seminole, Creek, and Cherokee. These tribes were friendly to the settlers. They learned to speak and read English. They wanted to live in peace. They became known as the "Five Civilized Tribes."

Unfortunately, these tribes had the land that the farmers wanted. The farmers asked the government to get the tribes off this land. The farmers didn't care about the native people. They just wanted the land.

1. Underline the sentence that tells what the farmers of the southeast wanted.

2. Underline the sentence that tells what the main tribes of the southeast became known as.

3. Underline the sentence that tells what the farmers asked the government to do.

Answer the questions with complete sentences.

1. Why was there trouble between the early settlers and the native tribes?

_____

_____

2. What did the farmers of the southeast want?

_____

_____

3. Who were the main tribes of the southeast?

_____

_____

4. What did the main tribes become known as?

_____

_____

5. What did the farmers ask the government to do?

_____

_____

Signing of the Indian Removal Act

In 1830, Andrew Jackson was president of the United States. He wanted to help the American farmers of the southeast. He wanted to give them millions of acres of native land. On May 28, 1830, Jackson signed the Indian Removal Act. This gave the government the power to force native tribes off their land. In return, the tribes would be given land in the west. This land was called Indian Territory.

Indian Territory

Indian Territory was west of the Mississippi River. This territory was part of the Louisiana Purchase. It was a large piece of land which is now the state of Oklahoma. No white settlers were allowed to live in Indian Territory. It was supposed to be a place where the Indians could live in peace. Most of the native people did not want to move there. They did not want to leave their homes.

Indian Treaties

The U.S. government made treaties, or agreements, with the "Five Civilized Tribes." The government agreed to give them money for their land. They gave the tribes new land in Indian Territory. They were supposed to give them food and supplies for the journey. Some members of the tribes were willing to go along with the treaties. But most tribal members did not like the treaties.

1. Underline the sentence that tells who signed the Indian Removal Act.
2. Underline the two sentences that tell where Indian Territory was located.
3. Underline the sentence that tells who the government made treaties with.

Name_____ Date_____

Answer the questions with complete sentences.

1. Who signed the Indian Removal Act?

   _____

   _____

2. What did the Indian Removal Act do?

   _____

   _____

3. Where was Indian Territory located?

   _____

   _____

4. Who did the U.S. government make treaties with?

   _____

   _____

5. How did most tribal members feel about the treaties?

   _____

   _____

The Removal Begins

The Choctaw were the first tribe forced to leave. They were leaving behind over 10 million acres in Mississippi. Their journey to Indian Territory was 400 miles. The people started leaving in the winter of 1830. Some of the Choctaw walked. Some rode in wagons. It was a very difficult trip. It was so cold that first winter that some people froze to death.

The next tribe forced to leave their homes were the Creek. Fifteen thousand Creek left for Indian Territory. Only 11,500 survived the journey.

The Trail of Tears

In 1835, about 16,000 Cherokee were living in Georgia. They were ordered to leave their land. A small group of Cherokee had signed a treaty with the U.S. government. They had traded all the Cherokee land for some money and new land in Indian Territory. The rest of the Cherokee were very angry. They did not agree with the treaty. By 1838, only about 2,000 Cherokee had left Georgia. They rest had refused to leave.

Soldiers were sent to force the Cherokee out of their homes. They made all

the men, women, and children march 1,200 miles to Indian Territory. It was a very long and miserable trip. About 4,000 people died from hunger and disease along the way. This terrible journey became known as "The Trail of Tears."

1. Underline the sentence that tells how long the Choctaw journey to Indian Territory was.

2. Underline the two sentences that tell what a small group of Cherokee had done.

3. Underline the sentence that tells how many Cherokee people died on the march to Indian Territory.

Answer the questions with complete sentences.

1. Who was the first tribe forced to leave their homes?

    _____

    _____

2. How many Creek survived the journey to Indian Territory?

    _____

    _____

3. What did a small group of Cherokee do?

    _____

    _____

4. How many Cherokee people died on the march to Indian Territory?

    _____

    _____

5. What did the terrible journey of the Cherokee become known as?

    _____

    _____

Complete each sentence with a word from the box.

tribal	care	farmers
Cherokee	west	Choctaw
signed	hunger	peace

1. The _____ wanted the best land for their farms.

2. "The Five Civilized Tribes" wanted to live in _____.

3. The farmers didn't _____ about the native people.

4. Andrew Jackson _____ the Indian Removal Act on May 28, 1830.

5. Indian Territory was _____ of the Mississippi River.

6. Most _____ members did not like the treaties.

7. The _____ were the first tribe forced to leave their homes.

8. Soldiers were sent to force the _____ out of their homes.

9. About 4,000 Cherokee died from _____ and disease.

Read each completed sentence to make sure it makes sense.

Write two or more sentences about each topic.

"The Five Civilized Tribes"

_____

_____

_____

_____

Indian Territory

_____

_____

_____

_____

"The Trail of Tears"

_____

_____

_____

_____

Texas Independence

In the 1820s, Texas was part of Mexico. There was a lot of open land in Texas. Stephen Austin represented a group of 300 American families. He asked the Mexican government if the families could settle in Texas. The Mexican government agreed.

Soon, many more American settlers were moving to Texas. They built towns and started businesses. They farmed the land. By the 1830s, more Americans were living in Texas than Mexicans. The Americans did not want Texas to be part of Mexico. They did not want to follow Mexican laws. They did not want to pay Mexican taxes. The Americans wanted Texas to be its own republic.

In 1833, General Antonio Lopez de Santa Anna was president of Mexico. He was angry that the Americans were not following Mexican laws. He said no more Americans could come to Texas. Santa Anna wanted Texas to stay part of Mexico. He sent soldiers to Texas. He wanted to stop the Americans from taking over. The Americans were very upset. They knew they would have to fight the Mexican soldiers. In 1835, the Americans set up their own government. Sam Houston became the Major General of the Texas army.

1. Underline the sentence that tells what Stephen Austin asked the Mexican government.

2. Underline the sentence that tells what was happening by the 1830s.

3. Underline the sentence that tells who General Antonio Lopez de Santa Anna was.

©Remedia Publications

Answer the questions with complete sentences.

1. What was Texas a part of in the 1820s?

    _____

    _____

2. What did Stephen Austin do?

    _____

    _____

3. What was happening in Texas by the 1830s?

    _____

    _____

4. Why did Santa Anna send soldiers to Texas?

    _____

    _____

5. Who was Sam Houston?

    _____

    _____

The Texas Revolution

There had been trouble between Mexico and the Americans in Texas for several years. In October of 1835, Santa Anna sent soldiers to Gonzales to get a cannon. He had given the cannon to the people of Gonzales. Now he wanted it back. The people of Gonzales refused to give back the cannon. They fired it at the soldiers. The soldiers left. This battle at Gonzales was the beginning of the revolution. The Texans wanted their independence from Mexico. And they were willing to fight for it!

The Alamo

In December, a rebel army of Texans drove Mexican troops out of San Antonio. The rebels took over the Alamo. The Alamo was just outside of San Antonio. It started out as a Spanish mission. Then it became a fort for Spanish and Mexican

soldiers. The Alamo was on three acres of land. The land was surrounded by a tall adobe wall. Inside the wall there was a chapel and a hospital. There were barracks for the soldiers. On top of the wall there were cannons.

Colonel James Bowie arrived at the fort in January of 1836. He had a group of about 30 men with him. Then Colonel William Travis came with about 140 soldiers. Davy Crockett and few men also showed up at the fort. Davy Crockett was known as the "King of the Wild Frontier." He wanted to help the Texans win their independence.

1. Underline the two sentences that tell what the people of Gonzales did.

2. Underline the sentence that tells who took over the Alamo.

3. Underline the sentence that tells what Davy Crockett wanted to do.

Name_____ Date_____

Answer the questions with complete sentences.

1. When Santa Anna sent soldiers to get a cannon, what did the people of Gonzales do?

   _____

   _____

2. Who took over the Alamo?

   _____

   _____

3. When did Colonel James Bowie come to the Alamo?

   _____

   _____

4. Who brought about 140 soldiers to the Alamo?

   _____

   _____

5. Why did Davy Crockett go to the Alamo?

   _____

   _____

The Battle of the Alamo

Santa Anna wanted to take back the Alamo. He gathered about 1,800 soldiers at the Rio Grande River. They started the long march towards San Antonio. Sam Houston heard about Santa Anna and his soldiers. He ordered everyone to leave the Alamo. James Bowie decided not to leave. He wanted to stay and defend the Alamo. William Travis and Davy Crockett stayed too. In the end, about 200 men stayed to fight the Mexicans.

Santa Anna arrived at the Alamo on February 23, 1836. Right away, the Texans started firing on the troops. Both sides fired at each other for 12 days. Santa Anna told the Texans to surrender or die. But they refused to surrender. This made Santa Anna very angry. He vowed to kill every man at the fort.

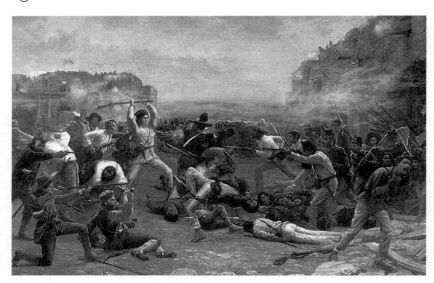

Early on March 6, Santa Anna ordered his men to surround the fort. The soldiers climbed over the wall. The Texans were outnumbered. They fought bravely but all of them were killed. About 600 Mexicans were also killed that day.

The Republic of Texas

Sam Houston wanted revenge. The Mexican army was at San Jacinto. Houston led about 900 Texans in a surprise attack. They shouted "Remember the Alamo!" This time the Texans won! They defeated the Mexican army. Santa Anna was captured. To save his life, Santa Anna gave Texas independence. Texas became the Republic of Texas.

1. Underline the sentence that tells what Sam Houston did after he heard about Santa Anna and his soldiers.

2. Underline the sentence that tells what Santa Anna told the Texans.

3. Underline the sentence that tells what Santa Anna did to save his life.

Answer the questions with complete sentences.

1. Why did Santa Anna gather soldiers at the Rio Grande River?

   _____

   _____

2. What did Sam Houston do after he heard about Santa Anna and his soldiers?

   _____

   _____

3. After both sides had been firing at each other for 12 days, what did Santa Anna tell the Texans to do?

   _____

   _____

4. What happened to the Texans that were defending the Alamo?

   _____

   _____

5. Why did Santa Anna give Texas independence?

   _____

   _____

Complete each sentence with a word from the box.

became	Alamo	bravely
save	part	ordered
cannon	independence	republic

1. In the 1820s, Texas was _____ of Mexico.

2. The Americans wanted Texas to be its own _____.

3. Sam Houston _____ the Major General of the Texas army.

4. The people of Gonzales fired the _____ at the soldiers.

5. A rebel army of Texans took over the _____.

6. Davy Crockett wanted to help Texas win their _____.

7. Sam Houston _____ everyone to leave the Alamo.

8. The Texans fought _____ but all of them were killed.

9. To _____ his life, Santa Anna gave Texas independence.

Read each completed sentence to make sure it makes sense.

Write two or more sentences about each topic.

The Alamo

_____

_____

_____

_____

General Antonio Lopez de Santa Anna

_____

_____

_____

_____

Sam Houston

_____

_____

_____

_____

The Mexican-America War: 1846–1848

Causes of the War

The Texas Revolution happened in 1836. Texas became a republic. In a republic, the citizens elect people to run the government. Sam Houston was elected the president of Texas. But the people of Texas didn't really want to be a republic. They wanted to be part of the United States. They asked Congress if Texas could become a state. It took Congress nine years to make a decision. Finally, in 1845, Texas became the 28th state of the United States of America.

The Mexican government was not happy. They did not want Texas to become a state. Santa Anna had given Texas its independence. But the Mexican government said Texas was still part of Mexico. They did not want America taking over Mexican land. Also, America and Mexico did not agree about the border of Texas. America thought the border was at the Rio Grande River. Mexico thought it was about 200 miles to the north. It was a big difference.

James Polk was president of the United States. He wanted America to have more land. At that time, Mexico owned a lot of territory in North America. Polk offered to buy some of that territory. Mexico did not want to sell. Instead, Mexico wanted to take back Texas.

1. Underline the sentence that tells what the people of Texas really wanted.

2. Underline the sentence that tells where America thought the border of Texas was located.

3. Underline the sentence that tells who the president of the United States was.

Name_____ Date_____

Answer the questions with complete sentences.

1. Why didn't the people of Texas want Texas to be a republic?

   _____

   _____

2. What did Mexico say about Texas?

   _____

   _____

3. Where did America think the Texas border was located?

   _____

   _____

4. What did President Polk want America to have?

   _____

   _____

   _____

5. What did Mexico want to do instead of sell their land?

   _____

   _____

Trouble at the Border

There were 3,000 Mexican troops at the Rio Grande River. They were protecting the border. Mexico did not want any Americans to cross the river. President Polk was mad at Mexico. He sent 4,000 American troops to the Rio Grande. General Zachary Taylor led the troops. Taylor settled his troops across from the Mexican troops. They stayed there for three months. Each side just watched each other. Then one day in April of 1846, shooting broke out. Some American soldiers were killed by Mexican troops. President Polk asked Congress to declare war on Mexico.

War Begins

Some people in Congress did not want war. They wanted America to live in peace. But by May of 1846, America was at war with Mexico. The American army was well-trained. They had new uniforms and modern weapons. They had plenty of food and water. The Americans were proud to be fighting for their country. The Mexican army had more men. But they were not very well trained. They had old weapons. Many soldiers did not even have uniforms. The Mexicans did not have enough to eat or drink. Most of the men had been forced by the government to become soldiers.

1. Underline the sentence that tells who led the American troops.
2. Underline the sentence that tells what President Polk asked Congress to do.
3. Underline the sentence that tells when America went to war with Mexico.

Answer the questions with complete sentences.

1. Who led the American troops to the Rio Grande?

    _____

    _____

2. Why did President Polk ask Congress to declare war on Mexico?

    _____

    _____

3. When did America go to war with Mexico?

    _____

    _____

4. Name two ways the American army was different from the Mexican army.

    _____

    _____

5. How did most Mexicans become soldiers?

    _____

    _____

One of the first battles was at Palo Alto. The Mexicans attacked first. They had a lot more men. But the American army won the battle. General Taylor moved his troops south into Mexico. In battle after battle, the Americans won. The Mexican soldiers fought bravely. But many of them were killed.

Santa Anna Returns

General Antonio Lopez de Santa Anna was a very famous Mexican general. Most Mexicans thought he was the only one who could beat the Americans. He had won some important battles for Mexico. He had also been president of Mexico. Then Santa Anna's enemies had kicked him out of the country. Now they wanted him back. Santa Anna came back to Mexico. He gathered and trained 15,000 troops.

In February of 1847, Santa Anna led all of his troops to Buena Vista. General Taylor was there with about 5,000 men. Santa Anna attacked the Americans. Both sides lost many men. The Americans were outnumbered. But they held their

ground. They won the battle. Even Santa Anna couldn't defeat the Americans.

The War Ends

Next the American army captured Mexico City. After that, the Mexican leaders surrendered. On February 2, 1848, a peace treaty was signed. The treaty included Mexico selling some of its land. President Polk paid them $15 million. He bought most of what is now Arizona, New Mexico, California, Colorado, Nevada, Utah, and Wyoming.

1. Underline the sentence that tells who Santa Anna was.

2. Underline the sentence that tells where Santa Anna led his troops.

3. Underline the sentence that tells when the peace treaty was signed.

Name_____ Date_____

Answer the questions with complete sentences.

1. What happened at the battle of Palo Alto?

    _____

    _____

2. Who was Santa Anna?

    _____

    _____

3. How many troops did Santa Anna have at Buena Vista? How many

    troops did General Taylor have?

    _____

    _____

4. Who won the battle of Buena Vista?

    _____

    _____

5. What happened after the American Army captured Mexico City?

    _____

    _____

Complete each sentence with a word from the box.

declare	Americans	back
captured	state	troops
modern	agree	defeat

1. Texas became the 28th _____ in 1845.

2. America and Mexico did not _____ about the
   border of Texas.

3. Mexico wanted to take _____ Texas.

4. General Zachary Taylor led the American _____
   to the Rio Grande.

5. President Polk asked Congress to _____ war on
   Mexico.

6. The American army had _____ weapons.

7. The _____ won the battle of Palo Alto.

8. Even Santa Anna couldn't _____ the Americans.

9. The Americans _____ Mexico City.

Read each completed sentence to make sure it makes sense.

©Remedia Publications

Write two or more sentences about each topic.

James Polk

_____

_____

_____

_____

General Zachary Taylor

_____

_____

_____

_____

Battle at Buena Vista

_____

_____

_____

_____

The Oregon Trail

After the Louisiana Purchase, America owned land west of the Mississippi River. Then America bought more western land from Mexico. The government wanted Americans to move to the western territory. They wanted America to stretch from the Atlantic to the Pacific Ocean. During the mid-1800s, the Oregon Trial was used by thousands of people traveling out west.

The People

The first western route was discovered by Lewis and Clark in the early 1800s. Fur traders and missionaries came next. The fur traders wanted to make money buying and selling furs. The missionaries wanted to bring Christianity to the native people. The fur traders and missionaries discovered what would become the Oregon Trail.

Marcus Whitman was a well-known missionary. He made the trip out west several times. With each trip he got closer to Oregon. Whitman took his wife and another missionary couple on one of his journeys. He wanted to prove that both men and women could make the trip to Oregon. This paved the way for others to follow.

Pioneer families were the next group to travel the Oregon Trail. Most early pioneers were farmers. They were looking for good farmland to raise cattle and grow crops. These American pioneers were very brave. They risked many dangers to have a better life.

1. Underline the sentence that tells how many people used the Oregon Trail.

2. Underline the sentence that tells who discovered what would become the Oregon Trail.

3. Underline the sentence that tells what most early pioneers were looking for.

Answer the questions with complete sentences.

1. During the mid-1800s, how many people used the Oregon Trail?

   _____

   _____

2. Why did missionaries travel out west?

   _____

   _____

3. Who discovered what would become the Oregon Trail?

   _____

   _____

4. What did Marcus Whitman want to prove?

   _____

   _____

5. What were most early pioneers looking for?

   _____

   _____

The Route

The Oregon Trail started in Independence, Missouri and ended in Oregon City, Oregon. It was about 2,000 miles long. It was a very difficult trail. The trail wound its way through Missouri. It went through parts of present-day Kansas, Nebraska, Wyoming, Idaho, and then into Oregon.

The Wagons

The pioneers traveled west in covered wagons. These wagons were like their moving vans. The wagons carried all their belongings. They carried everything the pioneers

would need to start a new life. The wagons were made of strong wood. They were very sturdy. They had a large wooden bed that was about 4 feet wide by 10 feet long. On top of the bed was a wood frame covered with canvas. The wagon had four big wooden wheels. Each wheel had an iron rim around the edge.

Furniture, bedding, clothing, household goods, and food were all packed into the wagons. Each family took hundreds of pounds of supplies. They bought flour, sugar, bacon, coffee, and salt to take with them. They had rifles and ammunition as well as farming tools. Each wagon had water barrels plus extra wheels and axles.

A team of horses, mules or oxen pulled the wagons. Most people used oxen. Oxen were strong and cost less money. They were easy to work with and could eat grass along the way.

1.   Underline the sentence that tells how long the Oregon Trail was.

2.   Underline the sentence that tells how the pioneers traveled west.

3.   Underline the two sentences that tell why most people used oxen to pull their wagons.

Answer the questions with complete sentences.

1. Name the present-day states that the Oregon Trail went through.

    _____

    _____

2. How did the pioneers travel west?

    _____

    _____

3. How big was the bed of a covered wagon?

    _____

    _____

4. What kind of food supplies did pioneers buy to take with them?

    _____

    _____

5. Why did most people use oxen to pull their wagons?

    _____

    _____

Wagon Trains

It was too dangerous for a family to travel alone. Instead, the pioneers traveled in wagon trains. Some wagon trains had up to 2,000 men, women, and children. There would be over 200 wagons. A herd of up to 5,000 cattle would be trailing behind the wagons. One person drove each wagon. Only the elderly or young children rode inside. Some people brought horses to ride. But most people walked along beside the wagons.

Each wagon train had a guide to lead the way. The wagon trains traveled between 10 and 20 miles a day. At night the wagons formed a huge circle for protection. Families would gather around campfires and cook dinner. They told stories and played music. Everyone was tired from the long day. But they were also excited to be starting a new life.

The Journey

The trip to Oregon took five or six months to complete. Planning for the trip could take up to a year. It was important to leave in April or May. The pioneers wanted to arrive before the winter snow. There were many dangers on this long journey. Some people got sick and died. Others were crushed under wagon wheels or were accidentally shot. Crossing rivers was especially dangerous. Wagons tipped over and supplies were lost. People and animals drowned. But somehow most people made it to their destination. They built homes and farmed the land. They began to settle the west.

1. Underline the sentence that tells how far the wagon trains traveled each day.

2. Underline the sentence that tells how long it took to travel to Oregon.

3. Underline the two sentences that tell why it was especially dangerous crossing rivers.

Name_____ Date_____

Answer the questions with complete sentences.

1. Why did pioneers travel in wagon trains?

   _____

   _____

2. How far did the wagon trains travel each day?

   _____

   _____

3. What did families do at night after the wagon train had formed a circle?

   _____

   _____

4. How long did it take to travel to Oregon?

   _____

   _____

5. Why was it especially dangerous crossing rivers?

   _____

   _____

Complete each sentence with a word from the box.

covered	traveled	beside
missionary	trip	protection
hundreds	pulled	pioneers

1. Thousands of people _____ on the Oregon Trail.

2. Marcus Whitman was a well-known _____ .

3. American _____ risked many dangers to have a better life.

4. Pioneers traveled west in _____ wagons.

5. Each pioneer family took _____ of pounds of supplies.

6. A team of horses, mules or oxen _____ the wagons.

7. Most people walked along _____ the wagons.

8. At night the wagons formed a huge circle for _____.

9. The _____ to Oregon took five or six months to compete..

Read each completed sentence to make sure it makes sense.

Write two or more sentences about each topic.

Pioneers

_____

_____

_____

_____

Marcus Whitman

_____

_____

_____

_____

Covered Wagons

_____

_____

_____

_____

Settling the West

Pioneer Life

Most pioneers on the Oregon Trail settled in Oregon. They became farmers in the Willamette Valley. There was lots of open land with rich soil. There was plenty of water and huge forests nearby. The first thing a pioneer family had to do was build a cabin. They cut down trees and made logs. The logs were stacked on top of each other to make the walls of the cabin. A mixture of mud sealed the cracks in the walls. Everyone in the family helped. While the cabin was being built, the family lived in their covered wagon.

Most log cabins were fairly small. Sometimes they were only 15 feet wide by 25 feet long. The whole family lived together in just one room. A large fireplace was built to keep the cabin warm. It was also used for cooking.

Usually the only furniture was a table, a few chairs, and some beds. All were made from wood.

The next big job was to clear the land around the cabin. Then the land had to be plowed. Once the land was plowed, crops were planted so there would be food to eat. Fences had to be built. The family also had to take care of the animals. Most people had cows, chickens, and horses. The work seemed to be never ending!

1. Underline the sentence that tells the first thing a pioneer family had to do.
2. Underline the sentence that tells where the family lived while the cabin was being built.
3. Underline the sentence that tells what happened after the land was plowed.

Answer the questions with complete sentences.

1. How were pioneer cabins made?

   _____

   _____

2. Where did the families live while their cabins were being built?

   _____

   _____

3. What was the fireplace used for?

   _____

   _____

4. What happened after the land was plowed?

   _____

   _____

5. What kind of animals did most people have?

   _____

   _____

Pioneer Families

Pioneer families needed to be large. Families with many children had more helpers. Families often included grandparents, aunts, uncles, and cousins. The adults and children worked from sunrise to sunset. Children had lots of chores. They collected firewood and fed the animals. They gathered eggs and took buckets to the river to get water. Girls helped with the sewing, cooking, and cleaning. Once the boys were old enough, they helped their fathers in the fields.

Frontier Towns

Business people went out west to build towns. They wanted to sell goods and services to the farmers. It was an opportunity to make

a lot of money. Early frontier towns were not fancy. They had dirt roads with just a few wooden buildings. There was usually a general store, a blacksmith, a shoemaker, and a barrel maker.

As more settlers arrived, the towns grew. Churches, schools, and banks were added. Nicer buildings were built. Some were made of brick. These larger towns attracted doctors, tailors, barbers, and other professionals. Homes were built for people who worked in town. Stagecoaches brought visitors and freight wagons brought supplies.

Since there were no close neighbors, farm life could be lonely. So going to town was a big social event. People could go to church, get supplies, visit with other families, and hear the local news.

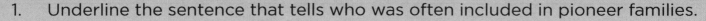

1. Underline the sentence that tells who was often included in pioneer families.
2. Underline the sentence that tells why business people went out west.
3. Underline the sentence that tells what people could do in town.

Answer the questions with complete sentences.

1. Who was often included in pioneer families?

   _____

   _____

2. What chores did girls help with? What did boys help with when they were old enough?

   _____

   _____

3. Why did business people go out west?

   _____

   _____

4. Describe what early frontier towns were like?

   _____

   _____

5. What could people do when they went to town?

   _____

   _____

Story 8

The Pony Express

Part of settling the west was getting mail to all the frontier towns. In early 1860, the mail was delivered by stagecoach. It took 24 days to get a letter from Missouri to California. Some Missouri businessmen had an idea for faster mail service. They called it the Pony Express. A route was chosen between St. Joseph, Missouri and Sacramento, California. This route covered about 1,900 miles. Over 150 relay stations were built along the route. Each relay station had several horses and a station keeper.

The idea was to fill special saddlebags with mail and put them on a horse. A rider would ride that horse as fast as possible for 15 to 20 miles. The rider would then stop at a relay station and get a fresh horse. Each rider rode about 75 miles per day. He might ride up to five different horses.

The Pony Express started in April of 1860. About 80 young riders were hired. There were over 400 horses. The riders were mostly teenage boys who weighed less than 125 pounds. The riders had to be light so that the horses could go fast. Now it took only 10 days to get mail delivered from Missouri to California!

The Pony Express lasted only 18 months. It went out of business because telegraph service became available. People could get messages in a few seconds. By 1869, the railroad brought the mail.

1. Underline the sentence that tells what each relay station had.
2. Underline the sentence that tells when the Pony Express started.
3. Underline the sentence that tells why riders had to be light.

Answer the questions with complete sentences.

1. How many relay stations were built along the Pony Express route? What did each station have?

   _____

   _____

2. How far did a Pony Express rider ride in a day?

   _____

   _____

3. When did the Pony Express start?

   _____

   _____

4. Why did Pony Express riders have to weigh less than 125 pounds?

   _____

   _____

5. How long did the Pony Express last?

   _____

   _____

Complete each sentence with a word from the box.

crops	services	faster
cabin	out	social
collected	riders	together

1. Everyone in the family helped to build the log _____.

2. The whole family lived _____ in just one room.

3. Once the land was plowed, _____ could be planted.

4. Children _____ firewood and gathered eggs.

5. Business people wanted to sell goods and _____ to the farmers.

6. Going to town was a big _____ event.

7. The Pony Express was a _____ mail service.

8. Pony Express _____ were mostly small teenage boys.

9. The Pony Express went _____ of business after only 18 months.

Read each completed sentence to make sure it makes sense.

©Remedia Publications 67   *Daily Literacy Activities: 19th Century American History*

Write two or more sentences about each topic.

Pioneer Cabins

_____

_____

_____

_____

Frontier Towns

_____

_____

_____

_____

The Pony Express

_____

_____

_____

_____

California Gold Rush

Discovering Gold

On January 24, 1848 gold was discovered at Sutter's Mill near Coloma, California. John Marshall was building a water-powered sawmill for John Sutter. As he was working, he found flakes of gold in the American River. Marshall got

very excited. He told Sutter about his discovery. The two men tried to keep it a secret. But, of course, word got out! Local newspapers wrote about it. They wrote about all of the gold at Sutter's Mill.

By the summer of 1848, most of the men living in San Francisco had left town. They were headed to the gold mines. Then men arrived by ship. Several thousand came to look for gold. They came from Hawaii, Mexico, Chile, Peru, and even China!

America had purchased California from Mexico in February of 1848. But the government didn't know about the gold. News of the discovery would not reach the east coast until December of 1848.

The '49ers Come to California

After that, the news quickly traveled across the United States. There was gold in California! Men all over the country borrowed money and sold their belongings. They left their families behind and spent their life savings. These men had gold fever. They wanted to get rich quick. Around 90,000 would-be gold miners poured into California during 1849. These people became known as the '49ers.

1. Underline the sentence that tells where gold was discovered.

2. Underline the sentence that tells when news of the discovery of gold reached the east coast.

3. Underline the sentence that tells how many would-be gold miners poured into California.

Name_____ Date_____

Answer the questions with complete sentences.

1. Where was gold discovered? How was it discovered?

    _____

    _____

2. How did the secret of the gold get out?

    _____

    _____

3. When did news of the discovery of gold reach the east coast?

    _____

    _____

4. Why did men all over the country borrow money, sell their belongings and leave their families behind?

    _____

    _____

5. What were the 90,000 would-be gold miners who poured into California in 1849 know as?

    _____

    _____

The Miners

It was not easy or quick to get to California. About half of the '49ers came by wagon train. The other half came by ship. Each of these journeys took several months. By now, news had traveled all over the world. People were coming from Europe, Asia, and even Australia. Most of these men had no experience in gold mining. But they had a strong desire to become rich.

The first gold was found near the base of the Sierra Nevada Mountains. The hopeful miners went to the Sierras to start their search. There was a lot of ground to cover. They searched for gold nuggets along many different rivers and streams. Most of the miners worked alone. They staked out an area as their own. The miners used picks and shovels. They dug through the gravel and dirt until they found pieces of gold. Much of the gold was pretty close to the surface. So they didn't have to dig too deep.

One of the most popular methods for finding gold was called "panning for gold." This method used a special pan. The miners put gravel and water into the pan. Then they shook the pan back and forth. Any gold mixed in with the gravel fell to the bottom of the pan.

1. Underline the sentence that tells how long each journey to California took.

2. Underline the sentence that tells where the miners searched for gold nuggets.

3. Underline the sentence that tells what one of the most popular methods of finding gold was called.

Answer the questions with complete sentences.

1. How did the '49ers get to California? How long did it take?

   _____

   _____

2. Where did the miners search for gold nuggets?

   _____

   _____

3. What did the miners use to dig through the gravel and dirt?

   _____

   _____

4. Why didn't the miners have to dig too deep to find the gold?

   _____

   _____

5. What was one of the most popular methods of finding gold called?

   _____

   _____

Most of the early miners did become rich. The gold was plentiful. But it still took a lot of hard work and luck to find it. The miners put in long hours every day. A miner could make ten times more money mining as he did working a regular job. During 1849, over $10 million in gold was taken from the ground. In today's money, that would be about $250 million!

Boomtowns

When gold was found, it was called a "gold strike." News of a gold strike could bring hundreds of miners rushing to that area. The miners moved in and set up mining camps. The camps usually turned into boomtowns. The miners needed supplies and services. Stores, hotels, saloons, and other businesses were quickly built.

Boomtowns were rough and rowdy places. They were dirty. The buildings were cheaply made. But no one cared what the town looked like. The miners spent a lot of money and the merchants got rich quick. That was all that mattered. Most boomtowns turned into ghost towns. When the gold was gone, everyone left.

After the Rush

The gold rush lasted from 1848 until 1855. During that time, over 300,000 people came to California. Around 12 million ounces of gold was mined. That would be worth over $20 billion today! After 1855, gold was harder to find. Most mining was done by companies using machines.

1. Underline the sentence that tells how much gold was taken from the ground in 1849.

2. Underline the sentence that tells what a boomtown was like.

3. Underline the sentence that tells how many people came to California during the gold rush.

Answer the questions with complete sentences.

1. How much more money could a miner make mining gold than

   working a regular job?

   _____

   _____

2. How much gold was taken from the ground in 1849?

   _____

   _____

3. What happened when there was news of a gold strike?

   _____

   _____

4. Describe what a boomtown was like.

   _____

   _____

5. How many people came to California during the gold rush?

   _____

   _____

Complete each sentence with a word from the box.

method	rich	alone
flakes	wagon	strike
rowdy	ghost	wrote

1. John Marshall found _____ of gold in the American River.

2. Local Newspapers _____ about gold at Sutter's Mill.

3. Would-be gold miners wanted to get _____ quick.

4. About half of the '49ers came by _____ train.

5. Most of the miners worked _____.

6. Panning for gold was a popular _____ for finding gold.

7. When gold was found, it was called a gold _____.

8. Boomtowns were rough and _____ places.

9. Most boomtowns turned into _____ towns.

Read each completed sentence to make sure it makes sense.

Write two or more sentences about each topic.

Sutter's Mill

_____

_____

_____

_____

Panning for Gold

_____

_____

_____

_____

Boomtowns

_____

_____

_____

_____

The Underground Railroad

Slavery in America

African slaves were first brought to America in the early 1600s. At first, slavery was legal in all of the 13 colonies. When colonists bought their farms and livestock, they also bought slaves. Slaves were thought of as property. Slaves did the hard labor on the farm. They plowed

the fields and planted the crops. Then they harvested the crops. Slaves were not treated well. They did not make any money. They were forced to live in terrible conditions. Slaves were not free people. They could not leave their owners.

America grew and the colonies became states. The number of slaves grew as well. By 1800, farmers in the northern states no longer had slaves. But the number of slaves in the South was close to a million. The southern states had many large plantations. Slaves were very important to plantation owners. Without the free labor, their plantations would not be a success. By 1860, there were four million African slaves in the South.

Abolitionists

Abolitionists were people who were against slavery. They felt slavery should be illegal in America. Some abolitionists made speeches against slavery. A newspaper called *The Liberator* had articles against slavery. In 1833, the American Anti-Slavery Society was formed in Philadelphia. Other antislavery groups were formed in cities and towns throughout the North.

1. Underline the sentence that tells when slaves were first brought to America.
2. Underline the sentence that tells how many slaves were in the South by 1860.
3. Underline the sentence that tells who abolitionists were.

Answer the questions with complete sentences.

1. What kind of jobs did slaves have to do on a farm?

    _____

    _____

2. How many slaves were in the South by 1860?

    _____

    _____

3. Why were slaves so important to plantation owners?

    _____

    _____

4. What is an abolitionist?

    _____

    _____

5. What was formed in 1833?

    _____

    _____

By 1846, slavery was illegal in most northern states. There also was pressure on the southern states to make slavery illegal. This made the plantation owners very angry. They would not give up their slaves.

Many slaves tried to escape from their owners. If they could just make it to the North, they would be free. At first, not very many succeeded. They were caught and punished. They were beaten and sometimes killed. The slaves who did make it started helping others escape. The abolitionist groups also wanted to help the slaves escape. Over time, the abolitionists organized a plan called the Underground Railroad. Part of the plan was an escape route. The route started in the South. Then it went into the northern states and up to Canada.

Stations and Stationmasters

The Underground Railroad wasn't a railroad with trains. But it did have stops called stations. These stations were all along the escape route. Escaping slaves could stay there and be safe. A station could be in an attic, a cellar, a closet or a secret room. Sometimes they were in a barn or a hidden tunnel. People who had stations in their homes, churches, or businesses were called stationmasters. It was dangerous to hide a runaway slave. Slave owners came after their slaves. They tried to catch them and take them back to the plantation.

1. Underline the sentence that tells what made the plantation owners very angry.

2. Underline the two sentences that tell about the escape route.

3. Underline the two sentences that tell where a station could be located.

Name_____ Date_____

Answer the questions with complete sentences.

1. Why were plantation owners in the southern states very angry?

   _____

   _____

2. What was the escape route for the Underground Railroad?

   _____

   _____

3. What were Underground Railroad stations used for?

   _____

   _____

4. Name some places a station could be located.

   _____

   _____

5. Who were the stationmasters?

   _____

   _____

Conductors

Conductors were men and women who helped the slaves get from one station to another. Conductors traveled to the South. From there they would meet with slaves who wanted to escape. Then they led the slaves along the escape route. A conductor's job was very dangerous. If caught, a conductor could be thrown in jail or even killed. The people of the South hated the Underground Railroad. They punished anyone caught helping their slaves escape.

The most famous conductor was Harriet Tubman. She had been born into slavery. She escaped to Philadelphia in 1849. Harriet made many trips back to the South. She was a very brave woman. She may have guided as many as 300 slaves to freedom!

Passengers

Runaway slaves, using the Underground Railroad, were called passengers. It took a lot of courage to make the decision to escape. The passengers had to travel hundreds of miles mostly at night. Much of their journey was on foot. They walked through thick forests. They had to cross deep rivers. The slave owners were chasing after them. There was the constant fear of being caught.

There are many stories of daring escapes. Between 50,000 and 100,000 slaves were helped by the Underground Railroad.

1. Underline the sentence that tells who conductors were.
2. Underline the sentence that tells who the most famous conductor was.
3. Underline the sentence that tells how many slaves were helped by the Underground Railroad.

Name_____ Date_____

Answer the questions with complete sentences.

1. Who were the conductors on the Underground Railway?

   _____

   _____

2. Who was Harriet Tubman?

   _____

   _____

3. What were runaway slaves using the Underground Railroad called?

   _____

   _____

4. How far did the passengers have to travel?

   _____

   _____

5. How many slaves were helped by the Underground Railroad?

   _____

   _____

Complete each sentence with a word from the box.

born	organized	illegal
property	meet	escape
after	southern	safe

1. Slaves were thought of as _____.

2. The _____ states had many large plantations.

3. Abolitionists felt slavery should be _____ in America.

4. Many slaves tried to _____ from their owners.

5. Abolitionists _____ a plan called the Underground Railroad.

6. Stations were places that slaves could stay and be _____.

7. Conductors traveled to the south to _____ with slaves who wanted to escape.

8. Harriet Tubman had been _____ into slavery.

9. Slave owners were chasing _____ the runaway slaves.

Read each completed sentence to make sure it makes sense.

Write two or more sentences about each topic.

Abolitionists

_____

_____

_____

_____

Underground Railroad Stations

_____

_____

_____

_____

Underground Railroad Conductors

_____

_____

_____

_____

The First Transcontinental Railroad

First American Railroads

The Baltimore and Ohio Railroad was the first railroad company in America. Construction on the first railroad tracks started in 1828. The first section of track was completed in 1830. It was only 13 miles long but it caused a lot of excitement.

By 1850, there was 9,000 miles of track throughout the northeast. There were dozens of local railroad lines. These railroads took passengers and freight from city to city.

Gold was discovered in California in 1848. Thousands of people were traveling out west. The only way to get to California was by wagon train or ship. Each of those journeys took several months. There was a great need for a transcontinental railroad. One that would connect the east coast with the west coast. A western journey by train would take only about a week.

The Transcontinental Route

Everyone agreed there should be a transcontinental railroad. Traveling out west by train would be faster, safer, and cheaper. But members of Congress disagreed about which route should be used. Northern politicians wanted to use a central route. Southern politicians wanted to use a southern route. The central route would start in Omaha, Nebraska, and end in Sacramento, California. The southern route would go through Texas, New Mexico, and Arizona. It would end in Los Angeles, California. Congress continued to argue about the route. Nothing happened for over 10 years!

1. Underline the sentence that tells how long the first section of railroad track was.

2. Underline the sentence that tells why everyone agreed there should be a transcontinental railroad.

3. Underline the sentence that tells which route the Southern politicians wanted to use.

Answer the questions with complete sentences.

1. When was the first section of railroad track completed? How long was it?

   _____

   _____

2. How long did it take to get to California by wagon or ship? How long would it take by train?

   _____

   _____

3. Why did everyone agree there should be a transcontinental railroad?

   _____

   _____

4. Why did Congress disagree about which route to use?

   _____

   _____

5. What was the difference in the central route and the southern route?

   _____

   _____

Pacific Railroad Act

There were serious problems between the northern and southern states. There were strong disagreements about slavery and other things. Sometimes the disagreements turned violent. In 1861, 11 Southern states decided to form a new nation. The South no longer wanted to be part of the United States of America.

Abraham Lincoln was president. The Civil War was just starting. It was a very unsettled time in America. But Congress still wanted to build the transcontinental railroad. The southern members of Congress were gone. The argument about the route was finally over.   So Congress quickly voted to use the central route. This route would need about 2,000 miles of track. In 1862, President Lincoln signed the Pacific Railroad Act.

The Pacific Railroad Act made it possible for work on the railroad to begin. The act said that the transcontinental railroad would have two main railroad companies. The Central Pacific Railroad would start in California. The Union Pacific Railroad would start in Nebraska. Their tracks would meet in Utah. The act also gave

the railroad companies land where they could build tracks. It gave them money for each mile of track built. Tracks that went over the mountains earned more money.

1. Underline the sentence that tells what 11 Southern states decided to do in 1861.

2. Underline the sentence that tells how much track was needed for the central route.

3. Underline the sentence that tells what made it possible for work on the railroad to begin.

Answer the questions with complete sentences.

1. What did 11 Southern states decide to do in 1861?

   _____

   _____

2. Why was the argument in Congress about the transcontinental route finally over?

   _____

   _____

3. How much track was needed for the central route?

   _____

   _____

4. What made it possible for work on the railroad to begin?

   _____

   _____

5. What were the names of the two companies that built the transcontinental railroad?

   _____

   _____

The Central Pacific Railroad

Story 11

The Central Pacific Railroad began laying track from Sacramento, California in 1863. Their route headed east and went over the Sierra Nevada Mountains. This route would be a huge challenge. Thousands of Chinese immigrants were hired to build the railroad. Nine tunnels had to be blasted through the mountains. It was very dangerous. Progress was slow. The men could only blast about one foot per day. They also had to deal with harsh winter weather. Between 500 and 1,000 Chinese died while doing this work.

The Union Pacific Railroad

The Union Pacific Railroad began laying track in 1865 from Omaha, Nebraska. Their route was mostly flat because it went west across the plains. Irish immigrants were hired to lay this track. It was still hard work. But they were able to complete about a mile of track per day. Cheyenne and Sioux warriors attacked the Irish as they worked. Part of the route went through Indian land. Many lives were lost.

The Railroad is Completed

On May 10, 1869, the two railroads finally met at Promontory, Utah. There was a big ceremony to celebrate the completion. California Governor Leland Stanford pounded in the final "golden spike." It was a dream come true! Now the east was linked to the west.

1. Underline the sentence that tells where the route for the Central Pacific Railroad went.

2. Underline the sentence that describes the route for the Union Pacific Railroad.

3. Underline the sentence that tells when the two railroads finally met.

Answer the questions with complete sentences.

1. Where did the route for the Central Pacific Railroad go?

_____

_____

2. Who was hired to build the railroad by Central Pacific?

_____

_____

3. Describe the route for the Union Pacific Railroad.

_____

_____

4. Who did Union Pacific hire to lay their track?

_____

_____

5. When and where did the two railroads finally meet?

_____

_____

Complete each sentence with a word from the box.

politicians	transcontinental	route
attacked	excitement	immigrants
California	faster	Utah

1. The first 13 miles of railroad track caused a lot of _____.

2. Traveling out west by train would be _____ , safer, and cheaper.

3. Southern _____ in Congress wanted to use a southern route.

4. Congress wanted to build the _____ railroad.

5. The central _____ would need 2,000 miles of track.

6. The Central Pacific Railroad would start in _____.

7. Chinese _____ were hired to build the railroad.

8. Cheyenne warriors _____ the Irish as they worked.

9. On May 10, 1869, the two railroads finally met in _____.

Read each completed sentence to make sure it makes sense.

©Remedia Publications

Write two or more sentences about each topic.

The Pacific Railroad Act

_____

_____

_____

_____

The Central Pacific Railroad

_____

_____

_____

_____

The Union Pacific Railroad

_____

_____

_____

_____

The Civil War: 1861–1865

The Civil War was the deadliest war in American history. Over 620,000 soldiers died. The Civil War was also called the "War Between the States." Americans fought against each other. Families, friends, and neighbors fought against each other. It was a terrible time for America.

Causes of the Civil War

By the mid-1800s, the Northern and Southern states were very different. The North had moved away from farming. People had moved to the cities. They worked in factories. They had a new way of life. Most people in the South still lived on farms. They did not want things to change.

The North and the South were deeply divided. Southerners believed in states' rights. They thought states should have more power than the federal government. Northerners disagreed. But the biggest problem was slavery.

Slavery was illegal in the North. Many people in the North thought slavery was evil. These people were called abolitionists. Abolitionists were working to end to slavery in America. The southern farmers were afraid. They did not want to give up their slaves. They depended on slave labor to grow their crops. Without slaves, their way of life would end.

Abraham Lincoln was elected president in 1860. Lincoln wanted a strong federal government. He was against slavery. Because of this, many southerners thought Lincoln was against the South.

1. Underline the sentence that tells how many soldiers died in the Civil War.

2. Underline the sentence that tells what the biggest problem was between the North and the South.

3. Underline the two sentences that tell why southerners thought Lincoln was against the South.

Answer the questions with complete sentences.

1. How many soldiers died in the Civil War?

   _____

   _____

2. How was the North different from the South in the mid-1800s?

   _____

   _____

3. What was the biggest problem between the North and the South?

   _____

   _____

4. Why did southern farmers not want to give up their slaves?

   _____

   _____

5. Why did southerners think Lincoln was against the South?

   _____

   _____

The Confederacy

Lincoln's election caused the South to take action. Within a few months, 11 southern states decided to form their own country. They did not want to be part of the United States of America anymore. Their new country was called the Confederate States of America or the Confederacy. The Confederacy had its own government and its own money. It had its own laws. The South would be free to keep its slaves. Jefferson Davis was elected president of the Confederacy. The North became known as the Union.

The Beginning of the Civil War

Lincoln was against the South leaving the United States. But he did not want war with the South. Lincoln said, "We are not enemies, we are friends." On April 12, 1861, Confederate soldiers attacked Fort Sumter in South Carolina. They made the Union soldiers at the fort leave. Lincoln could not ignore this. He called for volunteers to start fighting for the Union. The Civil War had begun!

Over 3 million men fought in the war. There were twice as many Union soldiers as Confederate soldiers. But the Confederate soldiers were very well-trained. They had some of the best commanders in America. They fought bravely and were determined to win. General Robert E. Lee led the Confederate forces. General Ulysses S. Grant led the Union forces.

1. Underline the sentence that tells what the new country the South formed was called.

2. Underline the sentence that tells what happened on April 12, 1861.

3. Underline the sentence that tells how many men fought in the war.

Answer the questions with complete sentences.

1. What did the South call the new country that they formed?

   _____

   _____

2. What happened on April 12, 1861?

   _____

   _____

3. What did Lincoln do after the Confederate soldiers made the Union soldiers leave Fort Sumter?

   _____

   _____

4. How many men fought in the Civil War?

   _____

   _____

5. Who led the Confederate forces? Who led the Union forces?

   _____

   _____

Life During the Civil War

Life was very hard during the war. Many of the men had gone off to fight. The women were left at home to support the families. In the north, women worked in factories, offices, and stores. In the South, the women had to run the farms and plantations. Women became nurses to help wounded soldiers. Women also helped the soldiers in other ways. They rolled bandages. They made blankets and ammunition. The South ran low on food. People often went hungry. Most of the fighting took place in the South. Cities and plantations were burned and destroyed. The southern people lived in fear.

The life of a soldier was horrible. Soldiers suffered many hardships. Often there was not enough food or water. During the fighting, thousands were killed. The injured soldiers did not get good medical treatment. More men died from disease and infection than from being shot.

The End of the Civil War

There were many bloody and violent battles during the four years of the war. Both sides had won major battles. But everyone was tired of fighting. Too many lives had been lost. The Civil War finally ended on April 9, 1865. General Lee surrendered to General Grant at the Appomattox Court House in Virginia. The South  had lost the war. Now it was time for America to find a way to be united again.

1. Underline the sentences that tell what happened to cities and plantations in the South.

2. Underline the sentence that tells what happened to injured soldiers.

3. Underline the sentence that tells when the war ended.

Answer the questions with complete sentences.

1. Why were the women left at home to support the families during the war?

   _____

   _____

2. What happened to the cities and plantations in the South?

   _____

   _____

3. What happened to injured soldiers during the war?

   _____

   _____

4. When did the Civil War finally end?

   _____

   _____

5. What did General Lee do at the Appomattox Court House in Virginia?

   _____

   _____

Complete each sentence with a word from the box.

nurses	fought	also
country	want	disease
elected	problem	surrendered

1. The Civil War was _____ called the "War Between the States."

2. The biggest _____ between the North and the South was slavery.

3. Abraham Lincoln was _____ president in 1860.

4. The South decided to form their own _____ .

5. Lincoln did not _____ war with the South.

6. Over 3 million men _____ in the war.

7. Women became _____ to help wounded soldiers.

8. More men died from _____ and infection than from being shot.

9. General Lee _____ on April 9, 1865.

Read each completed sentence to make sure it makes sense.

Write two or more sentences about each topic.

Abraham Lincoln

_____

_____

_____

_____

The Confederacy

_____

_____

_____

_____

General Robert E. Lee

_____

_____

_____

_____

Reconstruction of the South: 1865-1877 Story 13

During the Civil War, much of the South was destroyed. Most of the fighting took place in the southern states. Union soldiers burned down farms and plantations. They ruined fields and crops. The soldiers also burned some of the cities in the South. Now that the war was over, the Confederate government had fallen apart. Confederate money was not worth anything. The South was in bad shape.

Rebuilding the South

Reconstruction meant rebuilding the South. It meant helping the South to become part of the Union again. Union troops were sent to the southern states. They were there to make sure the southerners followed the new laws. And to make sure there was no more fighting. The government helped to rebuild roads  and cities. New schools were built. The North also helped southern farmers start growing crops again.

Each southern state had to rebuild its government. Then they had to be accepted back into the Union by Congress.

The Freed Slaves

The slaves were now free. But what about their future? Former slaves celebrated their freedom. They held meetings and parades. They asked to become citizens. They demanded the right to vote. The Freedmen's Bureau was set up to help with food and medical care. Many of the new schools were built for black children. For the first time, the children could get an education.

1. Underline the sentence that tells where most of the fighting took place.

2. Underline the sentence that tells what Reconstruction meant.

3. Underline the sentence that tells what the Freedman's Bureau was set up to do.

Answer the questions with complete sentences.

1. What happened to much of the South during the Civil War?

    _____

    _____

2. What did Reconstruction of the South mean?

    _____

    _____

3. Why were Union troops sent to the southern states?

    _____

    _____

4. Name two things the slaves did when they were freed.

    _____

    _____

5. What was the Freedman's Bureau set up to do?

    _____

    _____

The biggest challenge for the newly freed slaves was finding work. Some were given land to farm. But most of the land was given back to white Southerners. Many freed slaves ended up working for their former owners. They made very little money. They were not treated well.

New Laws

During Reconstruction, three new amendments were added to the U.S. Constitution. These were permanent laws of the land.

- The 13th Amendment made slavery illegal throughout the United States.
- The 14th Amendment made former slaves citizens of the United States. It said they were equally protected by the law.
- The 15th Amendment gave all male citizens, including African Americans, the right to vote.

The New Congress

To join the United States again, each state had to pledge its loyalty. They had to agree to follow the new laws. By 1870, all of the southern states were accepted back into the Union. Now each state could send representatives to Congress. Black men could vote! In 1867, the first African Americans were elected to public office in the South. During Reconstruction, hundreds of black men took part in local governments. Sixteen were elected to the U.S. House of Representatives. Two served as U.S. Senators.

The End of Reconstruction

Reconstruction ended in 1877. The Union troops left the South. After Reconstruction, the Northern leaders lost interest in equality for freed slaves. They let the southern states handle equal rights in their own way.

1. Underline the two sentences that tell what the 14th Amendment was.

2. Underline the sentence that tells what happened in 1867.

3. Underline the sentence that tells when Reconstruction ended.

Answer the questions with complete sentences.

1. Choose one of the three new amendments to the U.S. Constitution and tell what it does.

   _____

   _____

2. What did the southern states have to do to become part of the United States again?

   _____

   _____

3. What happened in 1867?

   _____

   _____

4. When did Reconstruction end?

   _____

   _____

5. What did Northern leaders do after Reconstruction ended?

   _____

   _____

Most southerners did not like the changes that happened during Reconstruction. Former slave owners were still angry about losing their slaves. After Reconstruction, black politicians were voted out of office. Southern states passed laws that limited what black people could do and where they could go. Laws were also passed that made it hard for black men to vote.

The Ku Klux Klan

The Ku Klux Klan was a secret group of white Southerners. The members were both rich and poor. They were professional men and laborers. The members wore hoods to hide their identity. The Klan's main goal was to scare black people and their white friends. They wanted to keep them from voting. The Klan did not want anyone voting for equal rights. They beat people and even killed them. The Klan burned down black churches and schools. They got away with this for many years. African Americans were afraid to vote. White southerners were afraid to be friends with black southerners.

Segregation

By the late 1800s, the South became segregated. Black people and white people were kept apart. White southerners thought they were better than black people. Laws were passed preventing black people from going to white restaurants or using white bathrooms. They could not go to the same schools, do the same jobs or shop in the same places as white people.

1. Underline the sentence that tells what happened to black politicians after Reconstruction.

2. Underline the two sentences that tell the main goal of the Ku Klux Klan.

3. Underline the sentence that tells when the South became segregated.

Name_____ Date_____

©Remedia Publications

Answer the questions with complete sentences.

1. What happened to black politicians after Reconstruction?

    _____

    _____

2. Who belonged to the Ku Klux Klan?

    _____

    _____

3. What was the main goal of the Ku Klux Klan?

    _____

    _____

4. When did the South become segregated?

    _____

    _____

5. Name two things black people could not do after segregation?

    _____

    _____

Complete each sentence with a word from the box.

Segregation	meant	freedom
former	right	even
out	Senators	burned

1. Union soldiers _____ down farms and

    plantations.

2. Reconstruction _____ rebuilding the South.

3. Former slaves celebrated their _____.

4. Many freed slaves ended up working for their _____

    owners.

5. The 15th Amendment gave black men the _____

    to vote.

6. Two African Americans served as U.S. _____.

7. Black politicians were voted _____ of office.

8. The Ku Klux Klan beat people and _____ killed

    them.

9. _____ kept black and white people apart.

Read each completed sentence to make sure it makes sense.

Write two or more sentences about each topic.

Freed Slaves

_____

_____

_____

_____

The Ku Klux Klan

_____

_____

_____

_____

Segregation

_____

_____

_____

_____

The Last of the Indian Wars

Story 14

The last of the Indian Wars took place between 1870 and 1890. The wars were mostly about the U.S. Army forcing Native Americans to live on Indian Reservations.

Indian Reservations

The U.S. government wanted America to grow. Government leaders decided to take over tribal land in the west. Reservations were created. Reservations were acres of land set aside for Native Americans. The native people were supposed to live on reservation land. Then settlers could live on native land.

Many Native Americans did not want to move to reservations. They fought to stay on their own land. There were many battles. Then the government started signing peace treaties with some of the tribes. The treaties said that the tribes would be paid for their land. But the tribes had to move to reservations. They had to agree to live in peace and not leave the reservations. The tribes were promised food, clothing, and medical help. The treaties also promised to protect reservation land from the settlers. Over time, many of the government's promises were broken. Tribal leaders stopped trusting the government to keep its word.

The Great Sioux Reservation

The Great Sioux Reservation included millions of acres of land. It was located in South Dakota and in a small part of North Dakota. In 1868, the Treaty of Fort Laramie was signed. The reservation became home to the Lakota Sioux and the Northern Cheyenne tribes.

1. Underline the sentence that tells what the Indian Wars were mostly about.

2. Underline the sentence that describes reservations.

3. Underline the sentence that tells why tribal leaders stopped trusting the government to keep its word.

Answer the questions with complete sentences.

1. What were the last Indian Wars mostly about?

   _____

   _____

2. Why were Indian Reservations created?

   _____

   _____

3. What did the peace treaties promise the tribes?

   _____

   _____

4. Why did tribal leaders stop trusting the government to keep its word?

   _____

   _____

5. Which tribes lived on the Great Sioux Reservation?

   _____

   _____

Events Leading to the Battle of the Little Bighorn

The land of the Great Sioux Reservation was supposed to be protected. The government had promised to keep it safe from outsiders. In 1873, the Northern Pacific Railroad started laying railroad tracks on part of the reservation. The government did nothing to stop this. The tribal leaders were very angry.

The Black Hills were part of the Great Sioux Reservation. In 1874, Lieutenant Colonel George Armstrong Custer and his men were sent to the Black Hills. They found large deposits of gold. Word got out that there was gold in the Black Hills. Hundreds of gold miners rushed to the area. The Sioux and Cheyenne watched as their land was invaded. The U.S. government had broken its treaty. They did not protect the reservation from the miners. The tribes felt betrayed by the government.

After this, many Sioux and Cheyenne decided to leave the Great Sioux Reservation. They joined Sitting Bull, Crazy Horse, and other rebel Sioux chiefs. These tribes had refused to live on the reservation. They had gone to Montana. Sitting Bull and Crazy Horse welcomed the people from the reservation. Now thousands of Sioux and Cheyenne were living in a large village by the Little Bighorn River.

1. Underline the sentence that tells what the Northern Pacific Railroad did in 1873.
2. Underline the sentence that tells what happened after word got out that there was gold in the Black Hills.
3. Underline the sentence that tells what the Sioux and Cheyenne did after they left the Great Sioux Reservation.

Answer the questions with complete sentences.

1.   What did the Northern Pacific Railroad do in 1873?

   _____

   _____

2.   What did Lieutenant Colonel Custer and his men find in the Black Hills?

   _____

   _____

3.   Why did hundreds of gold miners rush to the Black Hills?

   _____

   _____

4.   Why did the tribes feel betrayed by the government?

   _____

   _____

5.   What did the Sioux and Cheyenne do after they left the Great Sioux Reservation?

   _____

   _____

Battle of the Little Bighorn—Custer's Last Stand

The army heard about the large Indian village by the Little Bighorn. Soldiers were sent to force the Sioux and Cheyenne back onto the reservation. On June 26, 1876, Lieutenant Colonel Custer, Major Reno, and Captain Benteen led their troops to the Little Bighorn Valley. Reno and Benteen attacked the village with about 400 men. Several hundred warriors fought them off. About 50 soldiers were killed before the army retreated.

Custer had about 230 men with him. He started to attack the village. He was quickly stopped by about 2,000 warriors defending their families. The fighting was fierce. Custer's men were surrounded. Custer made it to a small hill with a few of his men. This is where he made his "last stand." Within an hour, Custer and all of his men were killed.

Wounded Knee Massacre

By 1890, all of the Sioux and Cheyenne had been forced onto reservation land. The people were suffering. They were starving and desperate. Some people started doing a Ghost Dance. The dance gave them hope for a better life. The U.S. government thought this was a war dance. The army was ordered to stop the Ghost Dancers.

First, Sitting Bull was arrested and killed. Then, a group of Ghost Dancers tried to escape. They were caught at Wounded Knee Creek. A fight broke out. Between 150 and 300 Lakota men, women, and children were killed by U. S. soldiers. This massacre was the last major conflict of the Indian Wars.

1. Underline the sentence that tells why soldiers were sent to the large Indian village by the Little Bighorn.
2. Underline the sentence that tells what happened to Custer and his men when he made his "last stand."
3. Underline the sentence that tells what happened after a fight broke out at Wounded Knee Creek.

Answer the questions with complete sentences.

1. Why were soldiers sent to the large Indian village on the Little Bighorn?

   _____

   _____

2. How many men did Custer have with him? How many warriors stopped Custer's attack on the village?

   _____

   _____

3. What happened to Custer and his men when he made his "last stand?"

   _____

   _____

4. Why was the army ordered to stop the Ghost Dancers?

   _____

   _____

5. What happened after a fight broke out at Wounded Knee Creek?

   _____

   _____

Complete each sentence with a word from the box.

reservation	men	tribal
betrayed	hope	fought
nothing	promises	massacre

1. Government leaders decided to take over _____ land in the west.

2. Native Americans _____ to stay on their own land.

3. Over time, many of the government's _____ were broken.

4. The government did _____ to stop the railroad.

5. The tribes felt _____ by the government.

6. Sitting Bull refused to live on the _____.

7. Within an hour, Custer and all of his _____ were killed.

8. The Ghost Dance gave people _____ for a better life.

9. The Wounded Knee _____ was the last major conflict of the Indian Wars.

Read each completed sentence to make sure it makes sense.

Write two or more sentences about each topic.

Lieutenant Colonel George Armstrong Custer

_____

_____

_____

_____

The Great Sioux Reservation

_____

_____

_____

_____

Sitting Bull

_____

_____

_____

_____

WORDS TO KNOW

Story 1   Lewis and Clark Expedition: The Beginning

astronomy	expedition	route	zoology
botany	expert	settlements	
Corps (kor)	hardships	territory	
eager	militia	vast	

Story 2   Lewis and Clark Expedition: The Journey

destination	harsh	keelboat
eventually	preparation	

Story 3   The War of 1812

cargo	anthem

Story 4   The Indian Removal Act

civilized	removal	treaties	tribal
unfortunately	government	miserable	

Story 5   Texas Independence

independence	republic	revenge	surrender
represented	refused	revolution	

Story 6   The Mexican-America War

agree	captured	defeat	protecting
border	citizens	elect	troops

Story 7   The Oregon Trail

Christianity	missionaries	pioneers
destination	oxen	protection

Story 8   Settling the West

available	relay	stagecoach
collected	saddlebags	telegraph

Story 9   California Gold Rush

boomtowns	plentiful	staked	rowdy

Story 10   The Underground Railroad

considered	plantations	illegal	passengers
determined	abolitionists	organized	

WORDS TO KNOW

Story 11   The First Transcontinental Railroad

argue	disagreements	immigrants	transcontinental
argument	earned	politicians	unsettled
construction	harsh	progress	violent

Story 12   The Civil War

abolitionists	destroyed	infection	volunteers
Confederate	determined	medical treatment	
Confederacy	elected	suffered	
deadliest	election	support	

Story 13   Reconstruction of the South

amendments	equality	permanent	rebuilding
destroyed	former	pledge	ruined
equal	identity	preventing	segregated
equally	loyalty	Reconstruction	segregation

Story 14   The Last of the Indian Wars

betrayed	fierce	promises	retreated
defending	massacre	rebel	
desperate	promised	reservations	

Story 1   Lewis and Clark Expedition: The Beginning

PEOPLE

Thomas Jefferson   Meriwether Lewis

European   William Clark

PLACES

Mississippi River   Pacific Ocean

Louisiana Territory   Virginia

France   Kentucky

Story 2   Lewis and Clark Expedition: The Journey

PEOPLE

Mandan

Sacagawea

Shoshone

PLACES

Missouri River   Fort Mandan

Rocky Mountains   Idaho

South Dakota   Snake River

North Dakota   Columbia River

Fort Clatsop

Story 3   The War of 1812

PEOPLE

James Madison

Andrew Jackson

Francis Scott Key

PLACES

Ohio River Valley   Northwest Territory

Canada   Chesapeake Bay

Fort Henry   Baltimore, Maryland

Washington, D. C.   Ghent, Belgium

New Orleans, Louisiana

Story 4   The Indian Removal Act

PEOPLE

Choctaw   Creek

Chickasaw   Cherokee

Seminole

PLACES

Oklahoma

Mississippi

Georgia

Indian Territory

Story 5   Texas Independence

PEOPLE
Stephen Austin
General Antonio Lopez de Santa Anna
Sam Houston
Colonel James Bowie
Colonel William Travis
Davy Crockett

PLACES
Texas
Gonzales
Rio Grande River
Alamo
San Antonio
San Jacinto

Story 6   The Mexican-America War

PEOPLE
James Polk
General Zachary Taylor

PLACES
Palo Alto
Bueno Vista

Story 7   The Oregon Trail

PEOPLE
Marcus Whitman

PLACES
Independence, Missouri
Oregon City, Oregon
Kansas

Nebraska
Wyoming
Idaho

Story 8   Settling the West

PLACES
Williamette Valley

St. Joseph, Missouri
Sacramento, California

Story 9   California Gold Rush

PEOPLE
John Marshall
John Sutter

PLACES
Sutter's Mill
Coloma, California

Hawaii
American River
Chile

Peru
China
Sierra Nevada
Mountains

Story 10   The Underground Railroad

PEOPLE
Harriet Tubman

Story 11   The First Transcontinental Railroad

PEOPLE
Abraham Lincoln
Governor Leland Stanford
Chinese
Irish

PLACES
Baltimore
Ohio
Omaha, Nebraska
New Mexico
Arizona
Sacramento, California
Los Angeles, California
Promontory, Utah

Story 12   The Civil War

PEOPLE
Jefferson Davis
General Robert E. Lee
General Ulysses S. Grant

PLACES
Fort Sumter
Appomattox Court House

Story 14   The Last of the Indian Wars

PEOPLE
Lietenant Colonel George Armstrong Custer
Major Reno
Captain Benteen
Lakota Sioux

Northern Cheyenne
Sitting Bull
Crazy Horse

PLACES
The Great Sioux Reservation
Black Hills
Little Bighorn River
Wounded Knee Creek

ENRICHMENT IDEAS

The following higher-level thinking skills questions can be used as discussion starters or as extended learning writing assignments.

1. How would you prepare if you were going on the Lewis and Clark Expedition? What kind of supplies would you want to take?

2. What do you think was the biggest challenge during Lewis and Clark's journey?

3. Do you think the United States should have gone to war with Britain in 1812?

4. Was the Indian Removal Act fair to the Native American tribes? Explain your answer.

5. If you had been at the Alamo, would you have stayed to fight or would you have left when Sam Houston ordered everyone to leave? Why?

6. Use your imagination to describe a day on the Oregon Tail.

7. How was pioneer life different from modern day life?

8. Do you think it was worth it for the '49ers to give up everything to look for gold? Explain your answer.

9. Explain how the Underground Railroad worked.

10. Why do you think the Underground Railroad was able to help slaves escape?

11. Why do you think President Lincoln did not want war with the South?

12. What do you think it was like to live in the South during Reconstruction?

13. Why do you think the U.S. government broke its treaties with the Native America tribes?

ENRICHMENT IDEAS

Find out more...

- Find out more about the route that Lewis and Clark traveled.

- Find out more about Sacagawea.

- Find out about Francis Scott Key.

- Find out more about the "Trail of Tears."

- Find out more about why Davy Crockett went to the Alamo.

- Find out more about the dangers of traveling on the Oregon Trail.

- Find out more about early frontier towns.

- Find out more about what it was like to be a gold miner.

- Find out more about Harriet Tubman.

- Find out more about the slaves that escaped using the Underground Railroad.

- Find out more about the Chinese immigrants who helped build the Transcontinental Railroad.

- Find out more about the Battle of Gettysburg.

- Find out more about General Robert E. Lee and General Ulysses S. Grant.

- Find out more about what happened to the freed slaves during Reconstruction.

- Find out more about Custer's Last Stand.

- Find out more about the Wounded Knee Massacre.

Story 1

Page 5
1. He wanted to increase the size of the country.
2. France owned the Louisiana Territory.
3. The Louisiana Territory was bought for $15 million.
4. Native American tribes lived in the territory.
5. He thought a water route to the Pacific Ocean might be found.

Page 7
1. He called it the Corps of Discovery.
2. He asked Meriwether Lewis.
3. He thought Lewis was a smart, brave person.
4. Lewis asked William Clark.
5. They met in the U.S. Army.

Page 9
1. It became known as the Lewis and Clark Expedition.
2. They built up their strength. They practiced survival skills. They made boats.
3. Lewis trained with top scientists. He studied botany, zoology, medicine, astronomy and map-making skills.
4. He bought food, clothing, camping equipment, medicine, rifles, and map-making tools.
5.He bought gifts for Native American tribes.

Page 10
1. increase 2. France 3. maps 4. expedition 5. expert 6. best
7. months 8. learned 9. supplies

Story 2

Page 13
1. Their mission was to explore the unknown Louisiana Territory.
2. They began their journey from St. Louis, Missouri.
3. The largest boat was 55 feet. It was used to carry supplies.
4. Sometimes the boats had to be pulled over rocks and rough spots. There were mosquitoes and ticks.
5. The expedition made it to South Dakota.

Page 15
1. The made friends with the Mandan people.
2. It was called Fort Mandan.
3. The men built canoes, made ropes and leather clothing. They learned from the Mandan.
4. She was an 18-year-old Shoshone girl.
5. She could be a guide and talk to the Shoshone. She could get them horses.

Page 17
1. It left in April of 1805.
2. Her brother helped because she was with the group.
3. They ate salmon and wild game.
4. It took them to the Pacific Ocean.
5. They brought back descriptions of plants and animals and a map of the route.

Page 18
1. mystery 2. journey 3. met 4. Mandan 5. fort 6. Shoshone
7. brother 8. reached 9. complete

Story 3

Page 21
1. They were using their ships to trade goods with other countries.
2. The British took American sailors from their ships and forced them to serve in the British navy.
3. It made the American government very angry.
4. The British wanted to stop Americans from settling in the Ohio River Valley.
5. The settlers asked the U.S. government for help.

Page 23
1. They voted to go to war on June 18, 1812.
2. The generals were inexperienced. The troops were unprepared. They ran out of supplies.
3. America got control of the Northwest Territory.
4. They fought back even harder. They sent more troops to America.
5. They burned government buildings including the White House.

Page 25
1. They thought if they could take the fort, they could win the war.
2. They fired for 25 hours.
3. Francis Scott Key wrote the poem.
4. They were tired of fighting.
5. Andrew Jackson won a big victory.

Page 26
1. shipping 2. sailors 3. attack 4. against 5. battles 6. burned
7. rockets 8. failed 9. treaty

Story 4

Page 29
1. The early settlers wanted the natives' land but the natives did not want to give it up.
2. They wanted the best land for their farms.
3. They were the Choctaw, Chickasaw, Seminole, Creek, and Cherokee.
4. They became known as the "Five Civilized Tribes."
5. The farmers asked the government to get the tribes off the land.

Page 31
1. Andrew Jackson signed the Indian Removal Act.
2. It gave the government the power to force native tribes off their land.
3. It was located west of the Mississippi in what is now the state of Oklahoma.
4. The government made treaties with the "Five Civilizes Tribes."
5. They did not like the treaties.

Page 33
1. The first tribe to leave was the Choctaw.
2. Only 11,500 Creek survived the journey.
3. They signed a treaty with the government trading all Cherokee land for some money and new land.
4. About 4,000 people died.
5. It became known as "The Trail of Tears."

Page 34
1. farmers 2. peace 3. care 4. signed 5. west 6. tribal 7. Choctaw
8. Cherokee 9. hunger

Story 5
Page 37
1. Texas was a part of Mexico.
2. He asked the Mexican government if American families could settle in Texas.
3. More Americans were living in Texas than Mexicans.
4. He wanted to stop the Americans from taking over.
5. Sam Houston became the Major General of the Texas army.
Page 39
1. They refused to give back the cannon and they fired it at the soldiers.
2. A rebel army of Texans took over the Alamo.
3. He came in January of 1836.
4. Colonel William Travis brought 140 soldiers.
5. Davy Crockett wanted to help the Texans win their independence.

Page 41
1. He wanted to take back the Alamo.
2. He ordered everyone to leave the Alamo.
3. He told the Texans to surrender or die.
4. They were all killed.
5. He was captured and he wanted to save his life.

Page 42
1. part 2. republic 3. became 4. cannon 5. Alamo
6. independence 7. ordered 8. bravely 9. save

Story 6
Page 45
1. They wanted it to be a state in the United States of America.
2. Mexico said Texas was still part of Mexico.
3. They thought it was at the Rio Grande River.
4. He wanted it to have more land.
5. They wanted to take back Texas.

Page 47
1. General Zachary Taylor led the troops.
2. Some American soldiers were killed by Mexican troops
3. America went to war with Mexico in May of 1846.
4. America had fewer men; they had new uniforms and modern weapons; they had plenty of food and water; they were well trained.
5. They were forced by the government to become soldiers.

Page 49
1. The Mexican army attacked first but the American army won the battle.
2. He was a very famous Mexican general.
3. Santa Anna had 15,000 troops. Taylor had 5,000 troops.
4. America won the battle.
5. The Mexican leaders surrendered.

Page 50
1. state 2. agree 3. back 4. troops 5. declare 6. modern
7. Americans 8. defeat 9. captured

Story 7
Page 53
1. Thousands of people used the Oregon Trail.
2. They wanted to bring Christianity to the native people.
3. Fur traders and missionaries discovered what would become the Oregon Trail.
4. He wanted to prove that both men and women could make the trip to Oregon.
5. The were looking for good farmland to raise cattle and grow crops.

Page 55
1. It went through Missouri, Kansas, Nebraska, Wyoming, Idaho, and Oregon.
2. They traveled in covered wagons.
3. It was about 4 feet wide and 10 feet long.
4. They bought flour, sugar, bacon, coffee, and salt.
5. Oxen were strong and cost less money. They were easy to work with and ate grass along the way.

Page 57
1. It was too dangerous to travel alone.
2. Wagon trains traveled between 10 and 20 miles a day.
3. Families would gather around the camp fire and cook dinner, tell stories, and play music.
4. It took five or six months.
5. Wagons tipped over, supplies were lost, people and animals drowned.

Page 58
1. traveled 2. missionary 3. pioneers 4. covered 5. hundreds
6. pulled 7. beside 8. protection 9. trip

Story 8
Page 61
1. Trees were cut down to make logs then the logs were stacked to make walls. The walls were sealed with with mud.
2. They lived in their covered wagon.
3. It was used to keep the cabin warm and for cooking.
4. Crops were planted so there would be food to eat.
5. Most people had cows, chickens, and horses.

Page 63
1. Grandparents, aunts, uncles, and cousins were included in pioneer families.
2. Girls helped with sewing, cooking, and cleaning. Boys helped their fathers in the fields.
3. They went out west to build towns.
4. They were not fancy. They had dirt roads with just a few wooden buildings.
5. People could go to church, get supplies, visit with other families, and hear the local news.

Page 65
1. There were over 150 relay stations. Each station had several horses and a station keeper.
2. He rode about 75 miles per day.
3. It started in April of 1860.
4. They had to be light so their horses could go fast.
5. It lasted only 18 months.

Page 66
1. cabin 2. together 3. crops 4. collected 5. services 6. social
7. faster 8. riders 9. out

Story 9
Page 69
1. Gold was discovered at Sutter's Mill near Coloma, California. John Marshall found it in the American River while he was working.
2. Local newspapers started to write about it.
3. It reached the east coast in December of 1848.
4. The had gold fever and wanted to get rich quick.
5. They were known as the '49ers.

Page 71
1. They came by wagon train and ship. It took several months.
2. They searched in many different rivers and streams.
3. They used picks and shovels.
4. Most of it was close to the surface.
5. It was called "panning for gold."

Page 73
1. He could make ten times more money.
2. $10 million worth of gold was taken from the ground.
3. Hundreds of miners moved to that area and set up mining camps.
4. A boomtown was rough and rowdy. It was dirty and the buildings were cheaply made.
5. Over 300,000 people came to California.

Page 74
1. flakes 2. wrote 3. rich 4. wagon 5. alone 6. method 7. strike
8. rowdy 9. ghost

Story 10
Page 77
1. They plowed the fields and planted and harvested the crops.
2. There were four million slaves.
3. Plantation owners needed free slave labor so their plantations would be a success.
4. An abolitionist is a person who is against slavery.
5. The Anti-Slavery Society was formed in 1833.

Page 79
1. There was pressure to make slavery illegal.
2. It started in the South and went through the northern states to Canada.
3. Escaping slaves could stay there and be safe.
4. A station could be located in an attic, a cellar, a closet, a secret room, a barn or a hidden tunnel.
5. They were the people who had stations in their homes, churches or businesses.

Page 81
1. They were the men and women who helped slaves get from one station to the next.
2. She was the most famous conductor.
3. They were called passengers.
4. They traveled hundreds of miles.
5. Between 50,000 and 100,000 slaves were helped.

Page 83
1. considered 2. southern 3. illegal 4. escape 5. organized
6. safe 7. meet 8. born 9. after

Story 11
Page 85
1. The first section of track was completed in 1830. It was 13 miles long.
2. It took several months by wagon or ship. It would take about a week by train.
3. It would be faster, safer, and cheaper to go out west by train.
4. The Northern politicians wanted to use a central route and the Southern politicians wanted to use a southern route.
5. The central route started in Nebraska and went to California. The southern route went through Texas, New Mexico, and Arizona and then to California.

Page 87
1. They decided to form a new nation.
2. The southern members of Congress were gone.
3. About 2,000 miles of track was needed.
4. The Pacific Railroad Act made it possible.
5. The Central Pacific Railroad and the Union Pacific Railroad built the railroad.

Page 89
1. It headed east and went over the Sierra Nevada Mountains.
2. Chinese immigrants were hired.
3. It was mostly flat because it went west across the plains.
4. They hired Irish immigrants.
5. The met on May 10, 1869 in Promontory, Utah.

Page 90
1. excitement 2. faster 3. politicians 4. transcontinental 5. route
6. California 7. immigrants 8. attacked 9. Utah

Story 12
Page 93
1. Over 620,000 soldiers died.
2. People in the North lived in cities and worked in factories. People in the South still lived on farms.
3. The biggest problem was slavery.
4. They depended on slaves to grow their crops. Their way of life would end without slaves.
5. Lincoln wanted a strong federal government and he was against slavery.

Page 95
1. They called their new country the Confederate States of America or the Confederacy.
2. Confederate soldiers attacked Fort Sumter.
3. Lincoln called for volunteers to start fighting for the Union.
4. Over 3 million men fought in the war.
5. General Robert E. Lee led the Confederate forces. General Ulysses S. Grant led the Union forces.

Page 97
1. Many of the men had gone off to fight.
2. The cities and plantations were burned and destroyed.
3. Injured soldiers did not get good medical treatment.
4. The war ended on April 9, 1865.
5. General Lee surrendered to General Grant.

Page 98
1. also 2. problem 3. elected 4. country 5. want 6. fought
7. nurses 8. disease 9. surrendered

Story 13
Page 101
1. Much of the South was destroyed.
2. It meant rebuilding the South and helping it become part of the Union again.
3. They were sent to make sure southerners followed the new laws and to make sure there was not fighting.
4. They celebrated their freedom. They held meetings and parades. They asked to become citizens and to be able to vote.
5. It was set up to help with food and medical care.

Page 103
1. 13th Amendment made slavery illegal. 14th Amendment made former slaves citizens and gave them equal rights. 15th Amendment gave all men the right the vote.
2. They had to pledge their loyalty and agree to follow the new laws.
3. The first African Americans were elected to public office.
4. Reconstruction ended in 1877.
5. They lost interest in equality for freed slaves.

Page 105
1. They were voted out of office.
2. White southerners who were both rich and poor, professional men and laborers belonged to the Klan.
3. The main goal was to scare black people and their white friends and keep them from voting.
4. It became segregated in the early 1800s.
5. They could not use white restaurants or bathrooms. They could not go to the same schools, do the same jobs or shop in the same stores as white people.

Page 106
1. burned 2. meant 3. freedom 4. former 5. right 6. Senators
7. out 8. even 9. Segregation

Story 14
Page 109
1. The wars were about the U.S. Army forcing Native Americans to live on Indian Reservations.
2. Reservations were created so that the government could take over tribal land.
3. They were promised food, clothing, medical care, and the protection of reservation land from settlers.
4. Many of the government's promises were broken.
5. The Lakota Sioux and the Northern Cheyenne tribes lived on the reservation.

Page 111
1. The railroad started laying railroad tracks on part of the reservation.
2. They found large deposits of gold.
3. Word got out that there was gold in the Black Hills.
4. The government did not protect the reservation from the miners.
5. They joined Sitting Bull and Crazy Horse and other rebel Sioux chiefs.

Page 113
1. They were sent to force the Sioux and Cheyenne back onto the reservation.
2. Custer had 230 men with him. Two thousand warriors stopped the attack.
3. Within an hour, Custer and all of his men were killed.
4. The government thought the Ghost Dance was a war dance.
5. Between 150 and 300 Lakota men, women, and children were killed by U.S. soldiers.

Page 114
1. tribal 2. fought 3. promises 4. nothing 5. betrayed
6. reservation 7. men 8. hope 9. massacre

NOTES

NOTES

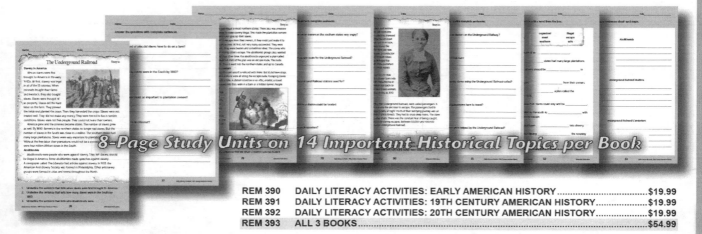